W9-CCT-253

CLASSIC WISDOM COLLECTION

TODAY'S QUESTIONS. TIMELESS ANSWERS.

Looking for time-tested guidance for the dilemmas of the spiritual life? Find it in the company of the wise spiritual masters of our Catholic tradition.

Way of Wonder

CLASSIC WISDOM COLLECTION

Way of Wonder

Wisdom from G. K. Chesterton

Compiled and with a foreword by Dale Ahlquist

BOOKS & MEDIA
Boston

Library of Congress Cataloging-in-Publication Data

Names: Chesterton, G. K. (Gilbert Keith), 1874-1936, author. | Ahlquist, Dale, editor.

Title: Way of wonder : wisdom from G.K. Chesterton / compiled and with an introduction by Dale Ahlquist.

Description: Boston : Pauline Books & Media, [2016] | Series: Classic wisdom collection | Includes bibliographical references.

Identifiers: LCCN 2015034937 | ISBN 9780819883605 (pbk.) | ISBN 0819883603 (pbk.)

Subjects: LCSH: Virtues--Religious aspects--Christianity. | Wonder--Religious aspects--Christianity.

Classification: LCC BV4630 .C48 2016 | DDC 230--dc23 LC record available at http://lccn.loc.gov/2015034937

The Scripture quotations contained herein are from the *New Revised Standard Version Bible: Catholic Edition,* copyright © 1989, 1993, Division of Christian Education of the National Council of the Churches of Christ in the United States of America. Used by permission. All rights reserved.

The selection of material by G. K. Chesterton that is not in public domain, copyright © 2016, The Royal Literary Fund. Used with permission.

Cover design by Rosana Usselmann

Cover photo: istockphoto.com/ © Daniel_Kay

"P "and PAULINE are registered trademarks of the Daughters of St. Paul.

Published by Pauline Books & Media, 50 Saint Paul's Avenue, Boston, MA 02130-3491

Printed in the U.S.A.

www.pauline.org

Pauline Books & Media is the publishing house of the Daughters of St. Paul, an international congregation of women religious serving the Church with the communications media.

1 2 3 4 5 6 7 8 9   20 19 18 17 16

Contents

Foreword

The most famous wise man in history said, "The fear of the LORD is the beginning of wisdom" (Prov 9:10). Three thousand years later, another wise man added, "But it is not the end." G. K. Chesterton (in his book on Saint Thomas Aquinas) plainly states what Solomon's proverb implies.

We approach God almost with a retreat. The first step toward the truth is made with such humble and holy reverence that it can only be described with the word "fear." The first encounter with truth is that we are unworthy of it. Our honest words are those of Saint Peter when he suddenly realized who Christ was: "Go away from me, Lord, for I am a sinful man" (Lk 5:8). That is the beginning of wisdom.

But it is not the end.

After we encounter God the Judge and reconcile with him, then we can properly encounter God the Creator. Chesterton says we can, even in a mystical way, be present at the moment of creation "when the foundations of the world are laid, with the morning stars singing together and the sons of God shouting for joy." (*Saint Francis of Assisi*).

The path to this fulfillment, this true joy, is paved by wonder. It is the sense of awe at something that is too good to be true—and yet is true. It is the path to holiness.

The natural response to revelation is wonder. Chesterton, the great writer of detective fiction and creator of the priest-sleuth Father Brown, enjoys the art of revelation, which usually means the startling solution at the conclusion of a mystery tale, or even the startling conclusion at the end of an essay. The surprise ending. But there is another technique in the mystery genre: that of revealing everything at the beginning, starting with what seems to be the perfect crime, one that will be impossible to solve, and then watching how the detective manages to solve it.

We could argue that the story of salvation has been told this way. We begin with the crime in the garden, the Fall that brings about death. It looks like death is going to be the victor. This great crime seems to be completed by an even greater crime, the death of God. But that turns out to be the solution. The death is a sacrifice. It is not the end, but the beginning. It leads to resurrection and the reward of eternal life. The central truth of our faith is indeed good news to a world mired in death and disobedience. We call those who proclaim this good news, this "gospel," evangelists. The story of salvation, just like the story of creation, is full of wonder.

Gilbert Keith Chesterton (1874–1936) is one of the most fascinating and delightful evangelists of the modern world. He was not a priest, not a preacher, not a member of a religious order. He was a British journalist, writing what he considered to be ephemera, and yet his "throwaway" words are still being read over seventy-five years after he laid down his pen and breathed his last. The words were written by a secular writer for a secular audience, yet new readers continue to be inspired by them, and as a result many of them have found their way to the Catholic Church.

One of the most prolific writers who ever lived, Chesterton was extremely popular in his own day. He wrote dozens of books on all subjects, as well as novels, plays, extensive poetry, and detective fiction. He was primarily a journalist and regularly contributed to both major and minor periodicals throughout his career. In constant demand as a speaker, he went on several lecture tours that took him throughout Europe, twice to America, and once to the Holy

Land. His conversion to Catholicism in 1922 was major news in the literary world, and most of his writing during the last decade of his life focused on the theory and practice of Catholic social teaching. Known for his aphorisms and good humor, he was widely quoted, and his opinions were sought on every topic of the day. The whole world mourned his death at the early age of sixty-two, and Pope Pius XI called him "a gifted defender of the Faith." Oddly, Chesterton went into an almost total eclipse after his death, but his work has begun to enjoy a revival in recent years. There is even a movement to see him canonized.

Chesterton's great challenge was to find a way to write about the ordinary in the world of journalism where only the things that are out of the ordinary are considered news: "I can say abnormal things in modern magazines. It is the normal things that I am not allowed to say" (*A Miscellany of Men*). And for Chesterton, the "ordinary" things are more important: "Ordinary things are more valuable than extraordinary things. Nay, they are more extraordinary" ("The Ethics of Elfland," *Orthodoxy*). And what are the ordinary things? They are the truths that are timeless, the truths that are eternal. "The most interesting ideas are those which the newspapers dismiss as dogmas" (*The Thing*). The fact that he managed to get these dogmas into the newspapers is one of his greatest accomplishments.

Though Chesterton considered himself to be nothing more than a journalist, his literary achievements far surpass that humble title. But he has not been served well by those who have tried to strictly categorize him as either a literary, or philosophical, or religious figure. He tried to be the representative, the voice of the common man, even if he was himself uncommon. And just as he does not fit well into any neat category, so the categories that I have chosen in order to present a selection from his writings are rather porous if not poor. But they show us, at least, the surprising connection between wonder and virtue.

It is safe to say that Chesterton presents not only classic wisdom, but condensed wisdom—great ideas packed into concise quotations. Though an incredibly prolific writer, he put the "ink" into "succinct." (Bear with me.) The mere taste of Chesterton's wisdom found in this small volume necessarily leaves out the complete meal. Missing is his profound treatment of evil; his magnificent quest for social justice; his original artistic, political, and historical insights; the full extent of his philosophical and theological understanding; and his detective fiction. While the overarching theme of this volume is wonder, Chesterton is one who finds great joy in doing battle, great joy in seeing justice achieved, great joy in solving the riddle. It is heartening to fight evil, to defeat what is wrong, to elevate what is right, and so it seems unfair to leave that part of Chesterton's message out, especially since his passion for justice filled so many pages of his writing. His compassion is twofold:

> As we should be genuinely sorry for tramps and paupers who are materially homeless, so we should be sorry for those who are morally homeless, and who suffer a philosophical starvation as deadly as physical starvation.

Excerpt from Illustrated London News,
November 24, 1934

But what is left out takes nothing away from the passages packed into this small volume. The choices here reflect those parts of the path to holiness that have drawn so many people to Chesterton—especially his wonder, his goodness, and his overflowing joy.

DALE AHLQUIST
President, American Chesterton Society

I

Wonder

Really, the things we remember are the things we forget. I mean that when a memory comes back sharply and suddenly, piercing the protection of oblivion, it appears for an instant exactly as it really was. If we think of it often, while its essentials doubtless remain true, it becomes more and more our own memory of the thing rather than the thing remembered. . . . This is the real difficulty about remembering anything: that we have remembered too much—for we have remembered too often. . . .

From this general memory about memory I draw a certain inference. What was wonderful about childhood is that anything in it was a wonder. It was not merely a world full of miracles; it was a miraculous world. What gives me this shock is almost anything I really recall, not the things I should think most worth recalling. This is where it differs from the other great thrill of the past, all that is connected with first love and the romantic passion; for that, though equally poignant, comes always to a point and is narrow like a rapier piercing the heart. Whereas the other was more like a hundred windows opened on all sides of the head.

—Excerpt from "The Man with the Golden Key," *Autobiography*

It is only the obvious things that are never seen; and a thing is often counted stale merely because men have been staring at it so long without seeing it. There is nothing harder to bring within a small and clear compass than generalizations about history, or even about humanity. But there is one especially evident and yet elusive thing in this matter of happiness. When men pause in the pursuit of happiness, seriously to picture happiness, they have always made what may be called a "primitive "picture. Men rush toward complexity, but they yearn toward simplicity. They try to be kings, but they dream of being shepherds.

—Excerpt from "The Moral of Stevenson," *Robert Louis Stevenson*

The world will never starve for want of wonders, but only for want of wonder.

—Excerpt from "Tremendous Trifles," *Tremendous Trifles*

We all feel the riddle of the earth, with no one to point it out for us.

—Excerpt from *William Blake*

Men, looking suddenly at spring flowers, have a poignant sense of being at once intoxicated and unsatisfied; a feeling only to be expressed in the words, "What is it all about?" What is that shining mystery which is called the beauty of the world? Who did it—why did they do it—what are they going to do next—what shall I do about it—what does it mean? What demanded explanation was not the process of vegetation but his interest in the process. It was not so much the question of a certain system in the world as of a certain spell laid upon him; and it may be noted that travelers and missionaries all report that in barbaric tribes the minimum of religion is always a belief in the charm or witchcraft of certain creatures or things. It was not the opening of the flowers the man wanted explained, but the opening of his own heart when he saw them. Religion did not begin in botany, but in psychology and aesthetics. The soul is satisfied, the soul only can be satisfied, by something involving a person or a story. Any explanation is good enough for grass, which today is, and tomorrow is cast into the oven.[1] But only one explanation is good enough for the beauty of grass. It is the explanation that springs to the lips of every good savage, of every good poet, and, I may add, of every good theologian. It is a God.

Then comes that next great leap of the liberated soul which the scientists cannot comprehend. The fascination of the flowers, when once it has touched the soul, demands a story and a person. The flowers were but a few hints that there *was* a story; and now the story has begun. For the soul cares . . . for the story of the spring—because it is a detective story.

A child does not look at the lustrous lattice-work of the frost, and say, "This can only be explained on the hypothesis that a man called Jack Frost does it with his finger." He feels that such feathery exactitude suggests the finger of somebody: and as he is not allowed, in the best regulated modern families, to say it is the finger of God; he says it is Jack Frost. The process which remains perfectly direct and prompt is the passage from the idea of beauty to the idea of personality: art cries out for an artist. It is plainly impossible that so standard a work as the universe should remain anonymous.

But when the child has thought of Jack Frost, he thinks more of Jack Frost than of the frost itself. The pattern only excites; but the person satisfies. By the end of the business, the child has begun to feel that Jack Frost has rather honored the windows by drawing on them at all. He is superior to windows, superior even to winter; he is what no dead things can be—he is in a story. As these children think about winter, so have all the children of men always thought about autumn and spring. If all this beauty meant purpose, the purpose took the first place; if not the beauty was hardly even beautiful. If the flowers meant a god, they were flung at the feet of the god. If they did not mean a god, they were flung away.

—Excerpt from *Daily News*, April 13, 1912

Unless the sky is beautiful, nothing is beautiful. Unless the background of all things is good, it is no substitute to make the foreground better.

—Excerpt from *New Witness*, October 12, 1916

A man's soul is as full of voices as a forest; there are ten thousand tongues there like all the tongues of the trees: fancies, follies, memories, madnesses, mysterious fears, and more mysterious hopes. All the settlement and sane government of life consists in coming to the conclusion that some of those voices have authority and others not. You may have an impulse to fight your enemy or an impulse to run away from him; a reason to serve your country or a reason to betray it; a good idea for making sweets or a better idea for poisoning them. The only test I know by which to judge one argument or inspiration from another is ultimately this: that all the noble necessities of man talk the language of eternity. When man is doing the three or four things that he was sent on this earth to do, then he speaks like one who shall live for ever. . . . There are in life certain immortal moments, moments that have authority.

—Excerpt from *Illustrated London News*, July 2, 1910

———— ✤ ————

At present the trend of the skeptical world is toward mere emancipation, accumulation, and enjoyment. Everyone is asking why they may not have this, why they should not do that. But anyone who knows the alphabet of man knows that happiness does not work like this, that a little goes a long way, that contrast counts for much—that people enjoy most the unexpected pleasure, the edges and the beginnings of things. In two words, we know that joy greatly depends on wonder; and we know that wonder partly depends on rarity.

—Excerpt from *Daily News,* March 2, 1907

The aim of life is appreciation; there is no sense in not appreciating things; and there is no sense in having more of them if you have less appreciation of them.

—Excerpt from "The God with the Golden Key," *Autobiography*

We should always endeavor to wonder at the permanent thing, not at the mere exception. We should be startled by the sun, and not by the eclipse. We should wonder less at the earthquake, and wonder more at the earth.

—Excerpt from *Illustrated London News*, October 21, 1905

All our educational experiments are in the wrong direction. They are concerned with turning children, not only into men, but into modern men; whereas modern men need nothing so much as to be made a little more like children. The whole object of real education is a renascence of wonder, a revival of that receptiveness to which poetry and religion appeal.

—Excerpt from *New Witness*, October 28, 1921

A child of seven is excited by being told that Tommy opened a door and saw a dragon. But a child of three is excited by being told that Tommy opened a door.

—Excerpt from "The Ethics of Elfland," *Orthodoxy*

And I know that clouds are alive and cling
     And the dusty path is rough
But I know that the least grain of dust
     Has never been praised enough.

—Excerpt from the poem "The Fanatic," 1920

We can only take a sample of the universe, and that sample, even if it be a handful of dust (which is also a beautiful substance), will always assert the magic of itself and hint of the magic of all things.

—Excerpt from "Paints in a Paint-box," *The Coloured Lands*

———— ❧ ————

Existence is still a strange thing to me, and as a stranger, I give it welcome.

—Excerpt from "The God with the Golden Key," *Autobiography*

———— ❧ ————

There is no such thing as an uninteresting subject; the only thing that can exist is an uninterested person.

—Excerpt from "On Mr. Rudyard Kipling and Making the World Small," *Heretics*

———— ❧ ————

Saint Francis . . . was above all things a great giver, and he cared chiefly for the best kind of giving which is called thanksgiving. If another great man wrote a grammar of assent, he may well be said to have written a grammar of acceptance—a grammar of gratitude. He understood down to its very depths the theory of thanks; and its depths are a bottomless abyss. He knew that the praise of God stands on its strongest ground when it stands on nothing. He knew that we can best measure the towering miracle of the mere fact of existence if we realize that but for some strange mercy we should not even exist.

—Excerpt from "The Testament of Saint Francis,"
Saint Francis of Assisi

The test of all happiness is gratitude. Children are grateful when Santa Claus puts in their stockings gifts of toys or sweets. Could I not be grateful to Santa Claus when he put in my stockings two marvelous legs? We thank people for birthday presents of cigars and slippers. Can I thank no one for the birthday present of birth?

—Excerpt from "The Ethics of Elfland," *Orthodoxy*

The point of the story of Satan is not that he revolted against being in hell, but that he revolted against being in heaven. The point about Adam is not that he was discontented with the conditions of the earth, but that he was discontented with the conditions of the earthly paradise.

—Excerpt from *New York American*, December 15, 1932

The sky is astonishing everywhere and should alone keep all men from materialism or indifference.

—Excerpt from "The Return of the Romans,"
The Resurrection of Rome

It is, after all, a precious and wonderful privilege to exist at all. . . . We must praise God for creating us out of nothing.

—Excerpt from "A History of Half-Truths," *Where All Roads Lead*

In the ultimate and universal sense I am astonished at the lack of astonishment.

—Excerpt from *New Witness*, January 25, 1917

The function of imagination is not to make strange things settled so much as to make settled things strange; not so much to make wonders facts as to make facts wonders.

—Excerpt from "A Defence of China Shepherdesses," *The Defendant*

The universe is a single jewel, and while it is a natural can't to talk of a jewel as peerless and priceless, of this jewel it is literally true. This cosmos is indeed without peer and without price: for there cannot be another one.

—Excerpt from "The Ethics of Elfland," *Orthodoxy*

What makes a real religion mystical is that it claims (truly or falsely) to be hiding a beauty that is more beautiful than any that we know, or perhaps an evil that is more evil. This gives another sort of intensity to common things, suggesting something that is redder than red, or more white than white.

—Excerpt from *Illustrated London News*, February 17, 1923

It is a strange thing that many truly spiritual men have actually spent some hours in speculating upon the precise location of the Garden of Eden. Most probably we are in Eden still. It is only our eyes that have changed.

—Excerpt from the Introduction, *The Defendant*

Can you not see that fairy tales in their essence are quite solid and straightforward, but that this everlasting fiction about modern life is in its nature essentially incredible? Folklore means that the soul is sane, but that the universe is wild and full of marvels. Realism means that the world is dull and full of routine, but that the soul is sick and screaming.

—Excerpt from "The Dragon's Grandmother," *Tremendous Trifles*

It is vain to learn to enjoy sport, or to enjoy art, or to enjoy festivity, if we have not learned the fundamental function: how to enjoy enjoyment.

—Excerpt from *Columbia*, October, 1924

There are no dreary sights; only dreary sightseers.

—Excerpt from "The Romance of the Marshes,"
Alarms and Discursions

I do not think there is anyone who takes quite such a fierce pleasure in things being themselves as I do. The startling wetness of water excites and intoxicates me: the fieriness of fire, the steeliness of steel, the unutterable muddiness of mud.

—Excerpt from a letter postmarked July 8, 1899,
to his fiancée, Frances

The mystic is not a man who reverences large things so much as a man who reverences small ones, who reduces himself to a point, without parts or magnitude, so that to him the grass is really a forest and the grasshopper, a dragon. Little things please great minds.

—Excerpt from *The Speaker*, December 15, 1900

The two facts which attract almost every normal person to children are, first, that they are very serious, and, secondly, that they are in consequence very happy. They are jolly with the completeness which is possible only in the absence of humor. The most unfathomable schools and sages have never attained to the gravity which dwells in the eyes of a baby of three months old. It is the gravity of astonishment at the universe, and astonishment at the universe is not mysticism, but a transcendent common sense. The fascination of children lies in this: that with each of them all things are remade, and the universe is put again upon its trial. As we walk the streets and see below us those delightful bulbous heads—three times too big for the body—which mark these human mushrooms, we ought always primarily to remember that within every one of these heads there is a new universe, as new as it was on the seventh day of creation. In each of those orbs there is a new system of stars, new grass, new cities, a new sea.

There is always in the healthy mind an obscure prompting that religion teaches us rather to dig than to climb; that if we could once understand the common clay of earth we should understand everything. Similarly, we have the sentiment that if we could destroy custom at a blow and see the stars as a child sees them, we should need no other apocalypse. This is the great truth which has always lain at the back of baby-worship, and which will support it to the end. Maturity, with its endless energies and aspirations, may easily be convinced that it will find new things to appreciate; but it will never be convinced, at bottom, that it has properly appreciated what it has got. We may scale the heavens and find new stars innumerable, but there is still the new star we have not found—that on which we were born.

But the influence of children goes further than its first trifling effort of remaking heaven and earth. It forces us actually to remodel our conduct in accordance with this revolutionary theory of the marvelousness of all things.

—Excerpt from "In Defence of Baby Worship," *The Defendant*

———❧———

There is at the back of all our lives an abyss of light, more blinding and unfathomable than any abyss of darkness; and it is the abyss of actuality, of existence, of the fact that things truly are, and that we ourselves are—incredibly and sometimes almost incredulously—real. It is the fundamental fact of being, as against not being; it is unthinkable, yet we cannot unthink it, though we may sometimes be unthinking about it; unthinking and especially *unthanking*. For he who has realized this reality knows that it does outweigh, literally to infinity, all lesser regrets or arguments for negation, and that under all our rumblings there is a subconscious substance of gratitude. That light of the positive is the business of the poets because they see all things in the light of it more than do other men. Chaucer was a child of light and not merely of twilight, the mere red twilight of one passing dawn of revolution, or the grey twilight of one dying day of social decline. He was the immediate heir of something like what Catholics call the Primitive Revelation; that glimpse that was given of the world when God saw that it was good. And so long as the artist gives us glimpses of that, it matters nothing that they are fragmentary or even trivial; whether it be in the mere fact that a medieval court poet could appreciate a daisy, or that he could write, in a sort of flash of blinding moonshine, of the lover who "slept no more than does the nightingale."[2] These things belong to the same world of wonder as the primary wonder at the very existence of the world; higher than any common pros and cons, or likes and dislikes, however legitimate. Creation was the greatest of all Revolutions. It was for that, as the ancient poet said, that the morning stars sang together; and the most modern poets, like the medieval poets, may descend very far from that height of realization and stray and stumble and seem distraught; but we shall know them for the Sons of God, when they are still shouting for joy. This is something much more mystical and absolute than any modern thing that is called optimism; for it is only rarely that we realize, like a vision of the heavens filled with a chorus of giants, the primeval duty of Praise.

—Excerpt from "The Greatness of Chaucer," *Chaucer*

We are the children of light, and [yet] it is we who sit in darkness.

—Excerpt from "A Defence of Patriotism," *The Defendant*

No, it is not that the world is rubbish and that we throw it away. It is exactly when the whole world of stars is a jewel, like the jewels we have lost, that we remember the price. And we look up as you say, in this dim thicket and see the price, which was the death of God.

—Excerpt from "The Tower of Treason,"
The Man Who Knew Too Much

II

Innocence

There was a time when you and I and all of us were all very close to God; so that even now the color of a pebble, the smell of a flower, comes to our hearts with a kind of authority and certainty; as if they were fragments of a muddled message, or features of a forgotten face.

—Excerpt from "Folly and Female Education,"
What's Wrong with the World

Men live . . . rejoicing—from age to age in something fresher than progress—in the fact that with every baby a new sun and a new moon are made.

—Excerpt from "The Two Voices," *The Napoleon of Notting Hill*

Babies are the most beautiful things on earth.

—Excerpt from "Christianity and Rationalism,"
The Blatchford Controversies

Children are innocent and love justice; while most of us are wicked and naturally prefer mercy.

—Excerpt from "On Household Gods and Goblins,"
The Coloured Lands

Because children have abounding vitality, because they are in spirit fierce and free, therefore they want things repeated and unchanged. They always say, "Do it again." And the grown-up person does it again until he is nearly dead. For grown-up people are not strong enough to exult in monotony.

But perhaps God is strong enough to exult in monotony. It is possible that God says every morning, "Do it again," to the sun; and every evening, "Do it again," to the moon.

—Excerpt from "The Ethics of Elfland," *Orthodoxy*

———

Innocence has about it something terrible which in the long run makes and re-makes empires and the world.

—Excerpt from the Introduction, *The Book of Job*

———

Knowledge and innocence are both excellent things, and they are both very funny. But it is right that knowledge should be the servant and innocence the master.

—Excerpt from the Introduction, *The Pickwick Papers*

———

Recent legislation has ridden roughshod over the instincts of innocent and simple, and yet very sensible people.

—Excerpt from "About Shamelessness," *As I Was Saying*

The maniac has lost more than innocence; he has lost essence, the complete personality that makes him a man.

—Excerpt from "On a Humiliating Heresy," *Come to Think of It*

The life of the wicked works outward and goes to waste. The life of the innocent, even the stupidly innocent, is within; if anyone dislikes the battered sentiment of the word "love," I will say that innocence has more zest, more power of tasting things.

—Excerpt from the Introduction, *Thackeray*

To be good and idiotic is not a poor fate, but, on the contrary, an experience of primeval innocence that wonders at all things.

—Excerpt from the Introduction, *Dombey and Son*

Nature worship is natural enough while the society is young, or, in other words, Pantheism is all right as long as it is the worship of Pan. But Nature has another side, which experience and sin are not slow in finding out, and it is no flippancy to say of the god Pan that he soon showed the cloven hoof. The only objection to Natural Religion is that somehow it always becomes unnatural. A man loves Nature in the morning for her innocence and amiability, and at nightfall, if he is loving her still, it is for her darkness and her cruelty. He washes at dawn in clear water as did the Wise Man of the Stoics,[1] yet, somehow at the dark end of the day, he is bathing in hot bull's blood, as did Julian the Apostate.[2] The mere pursuit of health always leads to something unhealthy. Physical nature must not be made the direct object of obedience; it must be enjoyed, not worshiped. Stars and mountains must not be taken seriously. If they are, we end where the pagan nature worship ended. Because the earth is kind, we can imitate all her cruelties. Because sexuality is sane, we can all go mad about sexuality. Mere optimism had reached its insane and appropriate termination. The theory that everything was good had become an orgy of everything that was bad.

—Excerpt from "The Flag of the World," *Orthodoxy*

⎯⎯⎯ ৵ ⎯⎯⎯

Man's primary purity and innocence may have dropped with his tail, for all we know. The only thing we all know about that primary purity and innocence is that we have not got it.

—Excerpt from "Science and Religion," *All Things Considered*

———— ❧ ————

The follower of Rousseau tended too much to say: "I am born in a state of innocence, and therefore I can be as guilty as I like." But the new skeptics, who also deny Original Sin, seem rather to be saying: "There is no Original Sin, because everybody can be born bad and behaves as badly as possible without it." The modern humanitarian believes in Total Depravity without any Fall to explain it.

—Excerpt from *New York American*, March 25, 1933

———— ❧ ————

Men do not become sinless by receiving a post in a bureaucracy.

—Excerpt from Preface to *Divorce vs. Democracy*

———— ❧ ————

The soul does not die by sin but by impenitence.

—Excerpt from "The Return of the Romans,"
The Resurrection of Rome

III

Goodness

The whole object of poetry and mysticism, the whole object of all religions and of all philosophies not invented by the devil, is to make us value good things.

—Excerpt from *Daily News,* December 24, 1904

❧

The highest thing in the world is goodness.

—Excerpt from "The True Vanity of Vanities,"
The Apostle and the Wild Ducks

❧

Every one of the popular modern phrases and ideals is a dodge in order to shirk the problem of what is good. We are fond of talking about "liberty"; that, as we talk of it, is a dodge to avoid discussing what is good. We are fond of talking about "progress"; that is a dodge to avoid discussing what is good. We are fond of talking about "education"; that is a dodge to avoid discussing what is good. The modern man says, "Let us leave all these arbitrary standards and embrace liberty." This is, logically rendered, "Let us not decide what is good, but let it be considered good not to decide it." He says, "Away with your old moral formulae; I am for progress." This, logically stated, means, "Let us not settle what is good, but let us settle whether we are getting more of it." He says, "Neither in religion nor morality, my friend, lie the hopes of the race, but in education." This, clearly expressed, means, "We cannot decide what is good, but let us give it to our children."

—Excerpt from "On the Negative Spirit," *Heretics*

A mother does not say to her child, "There is a personal God, the moral and Intelligent Governor of the universe." She says, "God will be pleased if you are good." She is quite as dogmatic as a college of theologians. Nay, she is more dogmatic, for it is more dogmatic to assume that a dogma is true than to declare that a dogma is true. But she is certainly simpler and better adapted for looking after babies than a college of theologians would be.

—Excerpt from *Daily News,* February 13, 1906

It is in the nature of man to find symbols outside himself of the qualities within himself. Thus, for instance, he has divided his virtues among the beasts of the field. He makes the lion represent bravery; yet men are braver than lions. No lions are ever burnt for their opinions. He makes the fox the type of cunning; yet men are more cunning than foxes. No fox has ever thought of getting on a horse's back so as to travel faster. He makes the ant a symbol of industry. He speaks of dog-like fidelity; it would be more emphatic to speak of man-like fidelity. Men are merrier than larks, and much more hypocritical than crocodiles. But we men cannot see ourselves as the great things that we are, and perhaps it is our greatness that we cannot. Perhaps this fantastic modesty is the highest of the attributes of man. Perhaps, amid the arrogance of oysters and the self-sufficiency of snails, man is the only humble animal.

—Excerpt from *Daily News,* March 21, 1906

There are only two ways of becoming more simple on the spot: one is to have a brick fall on your head and become suddenly quite childish; the other is to be quite extraordinarily good. Both of these methods are rather a nuisance.

—Excerpt from *Daily News,* February 8, 1908

If we are to be better than our fathers, we must at least be as good.

—Excerpt from *Daily News,* July 14, 1906

The ancient virtues are not the limits; they are, rather, the senses of the soul.

—Excerpt from *New Witness*, March 8, 1917

Every man's best virtues dwell in the dark.

—Excerpt from *Daily News,* July 2, 1901

Man is never genuinely at home except in goodness.

—Excerpt from *Daily News*, June 18, 1901

Right is right, even if nobody does it. Wrong is wrong, even if everybody is wrong about it.

—Excerpt from "Tom Jones and Morality,"
All Things Considered

The words *optimist* and *pessimist* seem to me so dubious and unphilosophical as to be all but useless; and if my [critic] likes to call me a good pessimist because I enjoy life, I shall not complain. That definition of a pessimist may be for all I know one possible use of a somewhat useless word. But there is another possible use of that word, for which I always myself employ it. If I am led by the accidental needs of language to use the word *pessimist*, I am quite willing to state what I mean by it. I use it as describing a man who regards the actual experience of existing, in its entirety as a thing not worth having. It is not in the least a question of whether there is more good or more evil in the world; it is a question of whether there is enough good, or good of such a kind as to create a definite interest in and attachment to the scheme of things.

The point for the pessimist is not that the world is a sort of work of art, and that through such and such defects it is bad. The point is not even that the world is not good; the point is that the world is a kind of investment, and that it is in the common business phrase "not good enough." If we attach this meaning to our vague word *pessimist*, it is perfectly evident that it has really very little to do with the degree or the energy of our denunciations of evil. A man does not become a pessimist however much he perceives evil. A man does not even become a pessimist however much he exaggerates evil. A man may make the world out much worse than it really is, and still retain that hilarious humility which is the only essential of our peace. A man may be a miserable man because he is sick of tragedies, or weary of interminable evil; he may be a miserable man, which is quite another thing, but he need not be a pessimist. An optimist may be sick of tragedy and weary of evil. He is only a pessimist when he is sick of happiness and weary of good.

—Excerpt from *Daily News*, December 30, 1905

It is the point of all deprivation that it sharpens the idea of value.

—Excerpt from "On Being Moved," *Lunacy and Letters*

———— ❦ ————

Every hateful thing is a mimicry of something that is good.

—Excerpt from *Illustrated London News*, June 15, 1912

———— ❦ ————

Of all the marks of modernity that seem to mean a kind of decadence, there is none more menacing and dangerous than the exaltation of very small and secondary matters of conduct at the expense of very great and primary ones, at the expense of eternal public and tragic human morality. If there is one thing worse than the modern weakening of major morals it is the modern strengthening of minor morals.

—Excerpt from "On Lying in Bed," *Tremendous Trifles*

———— ❦ ————

God himself will not help us to ignore evil, but only to defy and to defeat it.

—Excerpt from *Illustrated London News*, April 14, 1917

———— ❦ ————

This world can be made beautiful again by beholding it as a battlefield. When we have defined and isolated the evil thing, the colors come back into everything else. When evil things have become evil, good things, in a blazing apocalypse, become good. There are some men who are dreary because they do not believe in God; but, there are many others who are dreary because they do not believe in the devil.

—Excerpt from "On the Alleged Optimism of Dickens,"
Charles Dickens

A thing may be a good thing because it is a good medicine, but medicine implies a disease.

—Excerpt from *Illustrated London News*, September 4, 1920

The more we are certain what good is, the more we shall see good in everything.

—Excerpt from "Concluding Remarks," *Heretics*

We believe that you can have too much of a good thing—a blasphemous belief that at one blow wrecks all the heavens that men have hoped for.

—Excerpt from "The Pickwick Papers," *Charles Dickens*

God is not a symbol of goodness. Goodness is a symbol of God.

—Excerpt from *William Blake*

To see good is to see God.

—Excerpt from *The Listener*, January 4, 1933

IV

Purity

It seems to me that the mass of men do agree on the mass of morality, but differ disastrously about the proportions of it. In other words, all men admit the Ten Commandments, but they differ horribly about which is the first Commandment and which is the tenth. The difference between men is not in what merits they confess, but in what merits they emphasize. All the nations of the earth are troubled about many things; they only fight about what is the one thing needful. . . . Men do not differ much about what things they will call evils; they differ enormously about what evils they will call excusable.

—Excerpt from *Illustrated London News*, October 23, 1909

The act of defending any of the cardinal virtues today has all the exhilaration of a vice.

—Excerpt from "In Defence of a New Edition,"
The Defendant

Much has been said, and said truly, of the monkish morbidity, of the hysteria which has often gone with the visions of hermits or nuns. But let us never forget that this visionary religion is, in one sense, necessarily more wholesome than our modern and reasonable morality. It is more wholesome for this reason, that it can contemplate the idea of success or triumph in the hopeless fight toward the ethical ideal, in what Stevenson called, with his usual startling felicity, "the lost fight of virtue." A modern morality, on the other hand, can only point with absolute conviction to the horrors that follow breaches of law; its only certainty is a certainty of ill. It can only point to imperfection. It has no perfection to point to. But the monk meditating upon Christ or Buddha has in his mind an image of perfect health, a thing of clear colors and clean air. He may contemplate this ideal wholeness and happiness far more than he ought; he may contemplate it to the neglect or exclusion of essential things; he may contemplate it until he has become a dreamer or a driveler; but still it is wholeness and happiness that he is contemplating. He may even go mad, but he is going mad for the love of sanity. But the modern student of ethics, even if he remains sane, remains sane from an insane dread of insanity.

The anchorite rolling on the stones in a frenzy of submission is a healthier person fundamentally than many a sober man in a silk hat who is walking down Cheapside.[1] For many such are good only through a withering knowledge of evil. I am not at this moment claiming for the devotee anything more than this primary advantage—that though he may be making himself personally weak and miserable, he is still fixing his thoughts largely on gigantic strength and happiness, on a strength that has no limits and a happiness that has no end. Doubtless there are other objections that can be urged without unreason against the influence of gods and visions in morality, whether in the cell or street. But this advantage, the mystic morality must always have—it is always jollier. A young man may keep himself from vice by continually thinking of disease. He may keep himself from it also by continually thinking of the Virgin Mary. There may be questions about which method is the more reasonable, or even about which is the more efficient. But surely there can be no question about which is the more wholesome.

—Excerpt from "On the Negative Spirit," *Heretics*

Purity is the only atmosphere for passion.

—Excerpt from *G. F. Watts*

The great value of temperance is not that it increases restraint, but that it increases enjoyment.

—Excerpt from *Daily News,* December 24, 1904

The reward of chastity is a clearness of the intellect.

—Excerpt from "The Irishman," *George Bernard Shaw*

Mankind declares this with one deafening voice: that sex may be ecstatic so long as it is also restricted. It is not necessary even that the restriction should be reasonable; it is necessary that it should restrict. That is the beginning of all purity.

—Excerpt from *Illustrated London News*, January 9, 1909

And what, I ask you, is this modern worship of children? What, in the name of all the angels and devils, is it except the worship of virginity? Why should anyone worship a thing merely because it is small or immature?

—Excerpt from "An Interlude of an Argument," *The Ball and the Cross*

Much of the craving for novelty comes from the swiftness of satiety, and most of the swiftness of satiety comes from the restlessness of sin. And the whole Christian idea and imagery in these things, of being born again, of renewing our youth like the eagles, of becoming like little children, of drinking living water so that we never thirst again—all these things represent the idea that our ultimate triumph must be in gaining the power of never wearying, and not merely in always having something fresh of which to grow weary.

We all know that the Divine Authority itself selected the example of the child. We, most of us, know that this corresponds to a certain psychological fact even in our own experience; that some memories of childhood do have this very indescribable character of a positive and timeless pleasure. And this fact of psychology obviously fits in with the dogma of theology; it suggests that the more rapid exhaustion of our emotions is probably due to our more mature misuse of them.

Now I have treated this one point at some little length solely for the purpose of pointing out how awkward it is to introduce such a point into the vast and confused ignorance that is the atmosphere of modern controversy.

In the *Daily News* correspondence, I had to cram into a few lines—in a letter of a few paragraphs, which had to deal with this and six or seven other questions—this notion that the poetic attractiveness of childhood is really the heritage of the Christian idea that sin separates us from beatitude, and a witness to its truth; to the saying that the pure in heart can see God.

—Excerpt from *America*, August 11, 1928

I have seen speeches by solemn bishops and pompous schoolmasters which even identified physical cleanliness with ethical purity: they declared (in an ardor of self-admiration) that the English public schoolman is clean both inside and out. As if everybody did not know that, in the British Empire as much as in the Roman Empire, the dandies and the profligates take rather more baths than anybody else.

—Excerpt from *Illustrated London News*, April 30, 1910

We all disapprove of prostitution, but we do not all approve of purity. The only way to discuss the social evil is to get at once to the social ideal.

—Excerpt from "The Medical Mistake,"
What's Wrong with the World

———— ❧ ————

The pagans had always adored purity: Athene, Artemis, Vesta.[2] It was when the virgin martyrs began defiantly to practice purity that they rent them with wild beasts and rolled them on red-hot coals.

—Excerpt from "The Enemies of Property,"
What's Wrong with the World

———— ❧ ————

Perversity often comes out of the wrong sort of purity. Now it was the inmost lie of the Manichees[3] that they identified purity with sterility. It is singularly contrasted with the language of Saint Thomas, which always connects purity with fruitfulness, whether it be natural or supernatural.

—Excerpt from "A Meditation on the Manichees,"
Saint Thomas Aquinas

———— ❧ ————

There is the great contradiction that the modern person pretends to be at once too innocent and too sophisticated. First he says that certain sins are so remote and repulsive that only a low-minded spy would suspect their existence. Then he goes on to say that these sins are not so very bad, even if they exist. He shouts at the top of his voice: "To the pure in heart all things are pure," and then goes on to explain that there is really no such thing as purity.

—Excerpt from *Illustrated London News*, September 13, 1930

The man who said, "Blessed is he that expecteth nothing, for he shall not be disappointed," put the eulogy quite inadequately and even falsely. The truth is, "Blessed is he that expecteth nothing, for he shall be gloriously surprised." The man who expects nothing sees redder roses than common men can see, and greener grass, and a more startling sun. Blessed is he that expecteth nothing, for he shall possess the cities and the mountains; blessed is the meek, for he shall inherit the earth. Until we realize that things might not be, we cannot realize that things are.

—Excerpt from "Mr. Bernard Shaw," *Heretics*

I say a man must be certain of his morality for the simple reason that he has to suffer for it.

—Excerpt from *Illustrated London News*, August 4, 1906

Obedience is and has been often the most passionate form of personal choice. . . . If we believe in the sanctity of human life, it must be really a sanctity; we must make sacrifices for it, as the old creeds made for their sanctities. There must be no murdering of men wholesale because they stand in the path of progress. There must be no committing suicide because the landlady is unsympathetic and the books of Schopenhauer[4] impressive. If human life is mystical and of infinite value, murder must be really a crime. Suicide must be a greater crime than murder since it is the murder of the only man whose happiness we can appreciate. The faithful of the ancient creeds gave up, for the sake of their sanctities, the ultimate and imperious cravings of human nature—the desire of love and liberty and home. We profess to believe in the divinity of life, and we cannot give up for it a few grimy political advantages and a few sullen psychological moods. They gave up their joys, and we cannot even surrender lamentations. They denied themselves even the virtues of common men, and we cling openly, in art and literature, to the vices which are not even common. In this mood, we are not likely to open a new era.

—Excerpt from *Daily News,* December 3, 1901

———— ❧ ————

Men are never more awake to the good in the world than when they are furiously awake to the evil in the world. Men never enjoy so much the blazing sun and the rushing wind as when they are out hunting the Devil.

—Excerpt from *Daily News,* December 16, 1905

———— ❧ ————

White is a color; it is a shining and affirmative thing, as fierce as red, as definite as black. When, so to speak, your pencil grows red-hot, it draws roses; when it grows white-hot, it draws stars. And one of the two or three defiant verities of the best religious morality, of real Christianity, for example, is exactly this same thing; the chief assertion of religious morality is that white is a color.

Virtue is not the absence of vices or the avoidance of moral dangers; virtue is a vivid and separate thing, like pain or a particular smell. Mercy does not mean not being cruel or sparing people revenge or punishment; it means a plain and positive thing like the sun, which one has either seen or not seen. Chastity does not mean abstention from sexual wrong; it means something flaming, like Joan of Arc.

In a word, God paints in many colors, but He never paints so gorgeously—I had almost said so gaudily—as when He paints in white. In a sense, our age has realized this fact and expressed it in our sullen costume. For if it were really true that white was a blank and colorless thing, negative and non-committal, then white would be used instead of black and grey for the funeral dress of this pessimistic period.[5] We should see city gentlemen in frock coats of spotless silver linen with top hats as white as wonderful arum lilies, which is not the case.

—Excerpt from "A Piece of Chalk," *Tremendous Trifles*

White is indeed almost the definition of Paradise, since it means purity and also means freedom.

—Excerpt from "On Lying in Bed," *Tremendous Trifles*

Faith, Hope, and Charity

Every religion is a religion; that is, it ties a man to something. A faith can be free up to the exact point where it is unfaithful. . . . The truth is that if a man wishes to remain in perfect mental breadth and freedom, he had better not think at all. Thinking is a narrowing process. It leads to what people call dogma. A man who thinks hard about any subject for several years is in horrible danger of discovering the truth about it. . . . It is a terrible thing when a man really finds that his mind was given him to use and not to play with; or, in other words, that the gods gave him a great ugly mouth with which to answer questions, and not merely to ask them.

—Excerpt from *Illustrated London News*, September 16, 1909

———— ❧ ————

In our time there has come a quarrel between faith and hope—which perhaps must be healed by charity.

—Excerpt from "The Age of Legends," *A Short History of England*

———— ❧ ————

The only argument against losing faith is that you also lose hope—and generally charity.

—Excerpt from *Hearst's Magazine*, January 13, 1918

———— ❧ ————

Happiness is a state of the soul—a state in which our natures are full of the wine of an ancient youth; in which banquets last for ever, and roads lead everywhere; where all things are under the exuberant leadership of faith, hope, and charity.

—Excerpt from "Charles Dickens," *The Bookman*, 1903

———— ❧ ————

Faith is something superior to reason but not contrary to it.

—Excerpt from *Illustrated London News*, January 15, 1910

———— ✦ ————

Faith precedes all argument; I need not labor a point already laid down in Euclid. Euclid, that wild saint, cannot prove one proposition without getting us to agree with his assumptions.

—Excerpt from *Daily News,* July 16, 1904

———— ✦ ————

Whatever may be the meaning of faith, it must always mean a certainty about something we cannot prove.

—Excerpt from "Paganism and Mr. Lowes-Dickinson," *Heretics*

———— ✦ ————

The very things we cannot comprehend are the things we have to take for granted.

—Excerpt from "The Philosopher," *George Bernard Shaw*

———— ✦ ————

I believe (merely upon authority) that the world is round.

—Excerpt from *Daily News*, May 7, 1910

———— ༜ ————

I cannot work miracles, but I think it probable that there are some people who can . . . and I seem to remember somebody who (as I believe) could work miracles, but who was taunted in the hour of death with not working them, and taunted in vain.

—Excerpt from *Illustrated London News*, March 21, 1914

———— ༜ ————

When the old Christian dogmatic[1] said *"Credo quia Impossibile"*—"I believe it because it is impossible"—he was touching wittily a very deep truth.

—Excerpt from *Daily News*, May 9, 1903

———— ༜ ————

A man must take what is called a leap in the dark, as he does when he is married, or when he dies, or when he is born, or when he does almost anything else that is important.

—Excerpt from "W. W. Jacobs," *A Handful of Authors*

———— ❧ ————

Faith is that which is able to survive a mood.

—Excerpt from "The Orthodoxy of Hamlet," *Lunacy and Letters*

———— ❧ ————

No one worth calling a man allows his moods to change his convictions, but it is by moods that we understand other men's convictions. The bigot is not he who knows he is right; every sane man knows he is right. The bigot is he whose emotions and imagination are too cold and weak to feel how it is that other men go wrong.

—Excerpt from "The Anarchist," *Alarms and Discursions*

———— ❧ ————

Liberty is valuable that man may testify to his faith, not that he may turn away from it; liberty is to be preserved that we may preserve our convictions, not that we may lose them.

—Excerpt from *New Witness*, December 20, 1917

This is not an age of faith, but an age of credulity.

—Excerpt from *New Witness*, June 29, 1916

The iron racks of life . . . only an iron faith can endure.

—Excerpt from *Daily News,* February 15, 1901

Faith, of its own nature, wants to worship a real god.

—Excerpt from *Daily News,* November 9, 1912

Neither reason nor faith will ever die; for men would die if deprived of either.

—Excerpt from "Anti-Religious Thought in the 18th Century,"
The Spice of Life

The truth is that the tradition of Christianity (which is still the only coherent ethic of Europe) rests on two or three paradoxes or mysteries which can easily be impugned in argument and as easily justified in life. One of them, for instance, is the paradox of hope or faith—that the more hopeless is the situation the more hopeful must be the man.

—Excerpt from "The Moods of Mr. George Moore," *Heretics*

When I first read the *Penny Catechism*,[2] my mind was arrested by [the] expression that the two sins against hope are presumption and despair. . . . The heresies that have attacked human happiness in my time have all been variations either of presumption or of despair; which, in the controversies of modern culture, are called optimism and pessimism.

—Excerpt from "The History of a Half-Truth," *Where All Roads Lead*

Hope . . . is the thing that never deserts men and yet always, with daring diplomacy, threatens to desert them. It has indeed dwelt among and controlled all the kings and crowds, but only with the air of a pilgrim passing by. It has indeed warmed and lit men from the beginning of Eden with an unending glow, but it was the glow of an eternal sunset. . . . There is only one way in which it can even be noticed and recognized. If there be anywhere a man who has really lost it, his face out of a whole crowd of men will strike us like a blow. He may hang himself or become Prime Minister; it matters nothing. The man is dead.

—Excerpt from *G. F. Watts*

When the test of triumph is men's test of everything, they never endure long enough to triumph at all. As long as matters are really hopeful, hope is a mere flattery or platitude; it is only when everything is hopeless that hope begins to be a strength at all. Like all the Christian virtues, it is as unreasonable as it is indispensable.

—Excerpt from "The Mildness of the Yellow Press," *Heretics*

There is no real hope that has not once been a forlorn hope.

—Excerpt from "Schism of Nations," *A Short History of England*

Hope is the power of being cheerful in circumstances that we know to be desperate. It is true that there is a state of hope that belongs to bright prospects and the morning, but that is not the virtue of hope. The virtue of hope exists only in earthquake and eclipse.

—Excerpt from "Paganism and Mr. Lowes-Dickinson," *Heretics*

The happy reactionaries are blamed for their hopefulness.

—Excerpt from *Illustrated London News,* May 9, 1936

We insist that the ascetics were pessimists because they gave up threescore years and ten for an eternity of happiness. We forget that the bare proposition of an eternity of happiness is by its very nature ten thousand times more optimistic than ten thousand pagan saturnalias.[3]

—Excerpt from "Francis," *Varied Types*

It is currently said that hope goes with youth and lends to youth its wings of a butterfly; but I fancy that hope is the last gift given to man, and the only gift not given to youth.

Youth is pre-eminently the period in which a man can be lyric, fanatical, poetic; but youth is the period in which a man can be hopeless. The end of every episode is the end of the world. But the power of hoping though everything, the knowledge that the soul survives its adventures, that great inspiration comes to the middle-aged. God has kept that good wine until now.

—Excerpt from "The Boyhood of Dickens," *Charles Dickens*

I shall search the land of void and vision until I find something fresh like water and comforting like fire; until I find some place in eternity, where I am literally at home.

—Excerpt from "Authority and the Adventurer," *Orthodoxy*

It is the weakness of men to have far too much respect for the refinements of the class above them, and far too little charity for the coarser humors of the class below.

—Excerpt from *New Witness*, September 17, 1920

The things that go with good judgment [are] a sense of humor . . . charity [and] the dumb certainties of experience.

—Excerpt from "The Maniac," *Orthodoxy*

Charity is the imagination of the heart.

—Excerpt from *Illustrated London News*, March 11, 1911

Good charity is certainly better than bad criticism.

—Excerpt from *Daily News,* March 1, 1901

What is a beggar? A beggar is a man who asks help from another man solely in the name of something extraneous but common—as kinship or charity, the Fatherhood of God, or the brotherhood of man. He does not ask for the bread because he can at once give you the money, as in commerce. He does not ask for the bread because he will soon be able to pass you the mustard, as in society. He asks you for the bread because you are supposed to be under an ancient law of pity, by which (as it is written) if a man asks you for bread you will not give him a stone [see Mt 7:9]. That is what a beggar is. He is a man who begs—that is, he is a man who asks without any clear power of return, except the opportunity he offers you to fulfill your own ideals.

—Excerpt from *Illustrated London News*, February 25, 1911

Charity covers a multitude of sins—including uncharitableness.

—Excerpt from *Daily News,* July 21, 1906

Do not be kind merely to exhibit your own kindness; for that is an insult that is never forgiven. When you are helping people, pray for a spirit of humility; I had almost said, when you are helping them, pray for an appearance of helplessness.

—Excerpt from "On Bright Old Things—and Other Things," *Sidelights on New London and Newer York*

We make our friends; we make our enemies; but God makes our next-door neighbor. Hence he comes to us clad in all the careless terrors of nature; he is as strange as the stars, as reckless and indifferent as the rain. He is Man, the most terrible of the beasts. That is why the old religions and the old scriptural language showed so sharp a wisdom when they spoke, not of one's duty toward humanity, but one's duty toward one's neighbor. The duty toward humanity may often take the form of some choice which is personal or even pleasurable. That duty may be a hobby; it may even be a dissipation. We may work in the East End because we are peculiarly fitted to work in the East End, or because we think we are; we may fight for the cause of international peace because we are very fond of fighting. The most monstrous martyrdom, the most repulsive experience, may be the result of choice or a kind of taste. We may be so made as to be particularly fond of lunatics or specially interested in leprosy. . . . But we have to love our neighbor because he is *there*—a much more alarming reason for a much more serious operation. He is the sample of humanity which is actually given us. Precisely because he may be anybody, he is everybody.

—Excerpt from "On Certain Modern Writers and the Institution of the Family," *Heretics*

It is supposed that charity makes a man dependent; though in fact charity makes him independent, as compared with the dreary dependence usually produced by organization. Charity gives property, and therefore liberty. There is manifestly much more emancipation in giving a beggar a shilling to spend than in sending an official after him to spend it for him.

—Excerpt from "The Paradox of Labor," *Irish Impressions*

The fact that you extend Christian charity to murderers, to cannibals, or to cosmopolitan financiers, does not alter the fact that it is Christian charity you are extending and not humanitarian mildness, or skeptical toleration, or fatalist forbearance.

—Excerpt from *New Witness*, December 9, 1915

Charity is a paradox, like modesty and courage. Stated baldly, charity certainly means one of two things—pardoning unpardonable acts, or loving unlovable people. But if we ask ourselves (as we did in the case of pride) what a sensible pagan would feel about such a subject, we shall probably be beginning at the bottom of it. A sensible pagan would say that there were some people one could forgive, and some one couldn't: a slave who stole wine could be laughed at; a slave who betrayed his benefactor could be killed, and cursed even after he was killed. Insofar as the act was pardonable, the man was pardonable. That again is rational, and even refreshing, but it is a dilution. It leaves no place for a pure horror of injustice, such as that which is a great beauty in the innocent. And it leaves no place for a mere tenderness for men as men, such as is the whole fascination of the charitable.

Christianity came in here as before. It came in startlingly with a sword, and clove one thing from another. It divided the crime from the criminal. The criminal we must forgive unto seventy times seven. The crime we must not forgive at all. It was not enough that slaves who stole wine inspired partly anger and partly kindness. We must be much more angry with theft than before, and yet much kinder to thieves than before. There was room for wrath and love to run wild. And the more I considered Christianity, the more I found that while it had established a rule and order, the chief aim of that order was to give room for good things to run wild.

—Excerpt from "The Paradoxes of Christianity," *Orthodoxy*

The way to love anything is to realize that it might be lost.

—Excerpt from "The Advantages of Having One Leg,"
Tremendous Trifles

In the mystical triad of faith, hope, and charity, it is obvious that Christmas stands for charity, and among the more fortunate, for faith. Equally obviously, the New Year may well stand for hope.

—Excerpt from *Illustrated London News*, January 3, 1920

Charity means pardoning the unpardonable, or it is no virtue at all. Hope means hoping when things are hopeless, or it is no virtue at all. And faith means believing the incredible, or it is no virtue at all.

—Excerpt from "Paganism and Mr. Lowes-Dickinson," *Heretics*

VI

The Christian Ideal

If you wish for a sharp test to divide the true romantic from the false (a valuable thing when considering the claims of a poet, a son-in-law, or a professor of modern history), about the best I can think of is this: that the false romantic likes castles as much as cathedrals. If the poet or the lover admires the ruins of a feudal fortress as much as the ruins of a religious house, then what he admires is ruins; and he is a ruin himself. He likes medievalism because it is now dead, not because it was once alive; and his pleasure in the poetic past is as frivolous as a fancy dress ball. For the castles only bear witness to ambitions, to ambitions that are dead; dead by being frustrated or dead by being fulfilled. But the cathedrals bear witness not to ambitions but to ideals; and to ideals that are still alive. They are more than alive; indeed they are immortal because they are ideals that no man has ever been able either to frustrate or to fulfill.

—Excerpt from *Daily News,* May 27, 1911

If anything could possibly alter the balance of physical force it would be the spiritual ideals.

—Excerpt from *Daily News,* January 13, 1906

The Christian ideal has not been tried and found wanting. It has been found difficult and left untried.

—Excerpt from "The Unfinished Temple,"
What's Wrong with the World

Most Christians [fail] to fulfill the Christian ideal. This bitter and bracing fact cannot be too much insisted upon in this and every other moral question. But, perhaps, it might be suggested that this failure is not so much the failure of Christians in connection with the Christian ideal as the failure of any men in connection with any ideal. That Christians are not always Christian is obvious; neither are Liberals always liberal, nor Socialists always social, nor Humanitarians always kind, nor Rationalists always rational, nor are gentlemen always gentle, nor do working men always work. If people are especially horrified at the failure of Christian practice, it must be an indirect compliment to the Christian creed.

—Excerpt from *Daily News,* February 13, 1906

People will certainly say, "Seek your ideal house in the clouds; we have to build real houses with little enough money. See your ideal child in visions; we have to educate real children by thirty or forty at a time." To these I only answer that they have failed because of this "practicality." They have failed because, unlike hunters or fishers or even cobblers, they are not idealists. They start [out] expecting [things] to go wrong, which would ruin the aim of a rifleman. Because no man shoots quite straight, they abolish the bull's-eye. You cannot even make an imperfect thing unless you try to make a perfect one.

—Excerpt from *T. P.'s Weekly*, Christmas Number, 1909

It seems brazenly irrational that because people have failed to be Christians they should say that Christianity has failed. It might be mildly suggested to them that they need not look quite so far afield for the failure. My mother tells me not to climb a certain apple tree to steal apples, and I do it in spite of her. A bough breaks, a bulldog pins me by the throat, a policeman takes me to prison, whence I eventually return to shake my head reproachfully at my mother, and say in a sad and meditative manner; "I had hoped better things of you. Alas, there is something pathetic about this failure of motherhood to influence the modern mind; I fear we must all admit that maternity as an institution is barren and must be abandoned altogether." The impudence of this illogical shifting of responsibility is bad enough in the case of the Christian counsels of peace and pardon, in their strife against the human habits of vainglory and vengeance. But it is a thousand times more monstrous in the case . . . of the ideal of purity and the practice of profligacy. . . . Here, it seems, man is really to treat the religion like the imaginary mother; instead of blaming himself for not having obeyed her, he begins to abuse her for not having been obeyed. He first despises her advice and then despises her for giving advice that can be despised.

—Excerpt from *New Witness*, August 18, 1922

———✧———

The world really pays the supreme compliment to the Catholic Church in being intolerant of her tolerating even the appearance of the evils that it tolerates in everything else.

—Excerpt from "A Spiritualist Looks Back," *The Thing*

———✧———

A religion should not only be instinctively absorbent of whatever is consonant with its ideal; it should also be instinctively resistant to anything that is against that ideal. Men look to a faith to purge them of all native poisons, as well as to develop all native functions and pleasures. A church should have drainage as well as ventilation. It should drive bad smells out as well as let good smells in; it should not only cast out devils, but keep them out.

—Excerpt from *Daily News*, March 19, 1910

———✧———

Two types of reformers are fighting in the world today; those who strive to correct abnormal realities in conformity with a normal ideal; and those who wish to twist normal realities into conformity with an abnormal ideal. The first is in revolt because the common people are deprived of the common things. The second are also in revolt because it is hoped that they may learn to like uncommon things and to become uncommon people.

—Excerpt from *New Witness*, December 10, 1920

———— ❧ ————

I am quite ready to respect another man's faith; but it is too much to ask that I should respect his doubt, his worldly hesitations and fictions, his political bargain and make-believe.

—Excerpt from "The New Hypocrite,"
What's Wrong with the World

———— ❧ ————

A man who professes a creed confesses a partiality for the creed. When he loves it, he is necessarily partial. But when he hates it, he generally professes to be impartial. He pretends that the thing he hates is obstructing his way to other things; such as education or hygiene or science or social reform.

—Excerpt from *New Witness*, June 30, 1922

The man who picks out some part of Catholicism that happens to please him, or throws away some part that happens to puzzle him, does in fact produce, not only the queerest sort of result, but generally the very opposite result to what he intends.

—Excerpt from "The Optimist as a Suicide," *The Thing*

The skeptic has alternated between telling us to be true Christians and do it, and explaining that it is impossible to do.

—Excerpt from "The Mirror of Christ," *Saint Francis of Assisi*

When the art of controversy comes back, it will not come from the world of skeptics and iconoclasts. It will come rather from the world of believers and of dogmatists. It will not be the work of men who merely ask questions, but of men who believe that they have found answers. It will come out of the clash of real convictions, which are positive and not negative; not from those who say: "What is truth," but from those who can still say: "This is truth"; not from Pilate but from Paul.

—Excerpt from *New Witness*, September 8, 1922

When the world goes wrong, it proves rather that the Church is right. The Church is justified, not because her children do not sin, but because they do.

—Excerpt from "The Plan of This Book," *The Everlasting Man*

It is the reverse of all reason to suggest that a man's politics matter and his religion does not matter.

—Excerpt from "The Meaning of the Crusades,"
The New Jerusalem

In nothing does the Faith differ from the fads of the modern world more markedly than in this: that while it [Faith] calls for a great deal of self-control in all sorts of people for all sorts of reasons, there are really very few things which it absolutely forbids, as intrinsically and invariably evil; as having no higher form and no possible utility. Diabolism, the deformities of erotic perversion, the mere malice that delights in hurting others as such, the real blasphemy that is cold contempt of God, these are almost the only things I can think of. Love is lawful in marriage; wine is lawful in moderation; war is lawful in self-defense; gambling is lawful for those who can lawfully risk the money; and so on. That is exactly where Catholic morals do differ from the sweeping negations of the Pacifist and the Prohibitionist. The Catholic definition is carefully framed for freedom; to allow as much liberty and variety as is consistent with right reason.

—Excerpt from *Dublin Review,* Jan–Feb–Mar 1925

We are fighting not for Utopia but for Christendom; which defended itself through the Dark Ages of old, and would continue to defend itself even if the Dark Ages began anew.

—Excerpt from *New Witness*, August 5, 1921

If Christianity needs to be "new," it does not need to be Christian.

—Excerpt from *Illustrated London News*, June 19, 1915

I believe in that philosophy which claimed to come that we might have life, and that we might have it more abundantly. And I think it is because of our defects and disaffections that we weary of life, and not because life itself would not always be glorious to men truly alive.

—Excerpt from *Illustrated London News*, July 7, 1928

I believe that Christianity was a great vision of reality by people passing through a tragedy and confronted with death. When a man decides a thing on his death bed, it is taken for granted that he is serious. It is customary to be serious on one's death bed. Now while there are those who claim that the ancient world was dying and hardly itself when it decided in favor of Christianity, I am convinced by the nature of the men who were converted to Christianity that the ancient world was seriously convinced of the truth of Christianity. I am the more fortified in this view by knowing the claims of Christianity upon the mind to be very convincing.

—Excerpt from *Our Sunday Visitor*, August 2, 1931

I do believe in Christianity, and my impression is that a system must be divine which has survived so much insane mismanagement.

—Excerpt from *Illustrated London News*, October 6, 1906

Every man feels the faith or the sin.

—Excerpt from "W. E. Henley: Poet," *A Handful of Authors*

Christianity did *not* conceive Christian virtues as tame, timid, and respectable things. It *did* conceive of these virtues as vast, defiant, and even destructive things, scorning the yoke of this world, dwelling in the desert, and seeking their meat from God.

—Excerpt from "Monsters and the Middle Ages," *The Common Man*

Opponents of Christianity will believe anything except Christianity.

—Excerpt from *Illustrated London News*, January 13, 1906

The Church had learned, not at the end but at the beginning of her centuries, that the funeral of God is always a premature burial.

—Excerpt from "The Enigma of Waterloo,"
The Crimes of England

———— ❧ ————

To allow the horror of martyrdom to eclipse the halo of the martyr is simply a very stupid confusion of thought.

—Excerpt from *New Witness*, May 17, 1918

VII

Everyday Holiness

As I see the corn grow green all about my neighborhood, there rushes on me for no reason in particular a memory of the winter. I say "rushes," for that is the very word for the old sweeping lines of the plowed fields. From some accidental turn of a train journey or a walking tour, I saw suddenly the fierce rush of the furrows.

The furrows are like arrows; they fly along an arc of sky. They are like leaping animals; they vault an inviolable hill and roll down the other side. They are like battering battalions; they rush over a hill with flying squadrons and carry it with a cavalry charge. They have all the air of Arabs sweeping a desert, of rockets sweeping the sky, of torrents sweeping a watercourse. Nothing ever seemed so living as those brown lines as they shot sheer from the height of a ridge down to their still whirl of the valley. They were swifter than arrows, fiercer than Arabs, more riotous and rejoicing than rockets. And yet they were only thin straight lines drawn with difficulty, like a diagram, by painful and patient men. The men that plowed tried to plow straight; they had no notion of giving great sweeps and swirls to the eye.

Those cataracts of cloven earth; they were done by the grace of God. I had always rejoiced in them, but I had never found any reason for my joy. There are some very clever people who cannot enjoy the joy unless they understand it. There are other and even cleverer people who say that they lose the joy the moment they do understand it. Thank God I was never clever, and could always enjoy things when I understood them and when I didn't. I can enjoy the orthodox Tory,[1] though I could never understand him. I can also enjoy the orthodox Liberal, though I understand him only too well.

But the splendor of furrowed fields is this: that like all brave things they are made straight, and therefore they bend. In everything that bows gracefully there must be an effort at stiffness. Bows are beautiful when they bend only because they try to remain rigid, and [some] sword blades can curl like silver ribbons only because they are certain to spring straight again. But the same is true of every tough curve of the tree trunk, of every strong-backed bend of the bough; there is hardly any such thing in Nature as a mere droop of weakness. Rigidity yielding a little, like justice swayed by mercy, is the whole beauty of the earth. The cosmos is a diagram just bent beautifully out of shape. Everything tries to be straight, and everything just fortunately fails.

The foil may curve in the lunge, but there is nothing beautiful about beginning the battle with a crooked foil. So the strict aim, the strong doctrine, may give a little in the actual fight with facts; but that is no reason for beginning with a weak doctrine or a twisted aim. Do not be an opportunist; try to be theoretic at all the opportunities. Fate can be trusted to do all the opportunist part of it. Do not try to bend, any more than the trees try to bend. Try to grow straight, and life will bend you.

—Excerpt from "The Furrows," *Alarms and Discursions*

A man's philosophy of the cosmos is directly concerned in every act of his life. Call theories threads of cotton; still the strain of life is on these threads.

—Excerpt from *Daily News*, February 13, 1906

The Faith gives a man back his body, and his soul, and his reason, and his will, and his very life. . . . The man who has received it receives all the old human functions that all the other philosophies are already taking away.

—Excerpt from "The Sceptic as a Critic," *The Thing*

Man found it natural to worship. . . . He not only felt freer when he bent; he actually felt taller when he bowed. Henceforth, anything that took away the gesture of worship would stunt and even maim him forever. Henceforth, being merely secular would be a servitude and an inhibition. If man cannot pray, he is gagged; if he cannot kneel, he is in irons.

—Excerpt from "Man and Mythologies,"
The Everlasting Man

It is perfectly true that there is something in all good things that is beyond all speech or figure of speech. But it is also true that there is in all good things a perpetual desire for expression and concrete embodiment; and though the attempt to embody it is always inadequate, the attempt is always made. If the idea does not seek to be the word, the chances are that it is an evil idea. If the word is not made flesh, it is a bad word.

Thus Giotto or Fra Angelico[2] would have at once admitted theologically that God was too good to be painted, but they would always try to paint him. And they felt (very rightly) that representing him as a rather quaint old man with a gold crown and a white beard, like a king of the elves, was less profane than resisting the sacred impulse to express him in some way. That is why the Christian world is full of gaudy pictures and twisted statues which seem, to many refined persons, more blasphemous than the secret volumes of an atheist. The trend of good is always toward Incarnation.

But, on the other hand, those refined thinkers who worship the Devil, whether in the swamps of Jamaica or the salons of Paris, always insist upon the shapelessness, the wordlessness, the unutterable character of the abomination. They call him "horror of emptiness," as did the black witch in Stevenson's *Dynamiter*; they worship him as the unspeakable name; as the unbearable silence. They think of him as the unbearable silence. They think of him as the void in the heart of the whirlwind; the cloud on the brain of the maniac; the toppling turrets of vertigo or the endless corridors of nightmare. It was the Christians who gave the Devil a grotesque and energetic outline, with sharp horns and spiked tail. It was the saints who drew Satan as comic and even lively. The Satanists never drew him at all.

And as it is with moral good and evil, so it is also with mental clarity and mental confusion. There is one very valid test by which we may separate genuine, if perverse and unbalanced, originality and revolt from mere impudent innovation and bluff. The man who really thinks he has an idea will always try to explain that idea. The charlatan who has no idea will always confine himself to explaining that it is much too subtle to be explained. The first idea may really be very *outrée* or specialist; it may really be very difficult to express to ordinary people. But because the man is trying to express it, it is most probable that there is something in it, after all. The honest man is he who is always trying to utter the unutterable, to describe the indescribable; but the quack lives not by plunging into mystery, but by refusing to come out of it.

—Excerpt from "The Mystagogue," *A Miscellany of Men*

The whole question in which the existence of religion is involved is whether, while we have feelings about the catastrophic, we are or are not to have feelings about the normal; that, while we curse our luck for a house on fire, we are to thank anything for a house. If we come upon a dead man, we start back in horror. Are we not to start with any generous emotion when we come upon a living man, that far greater mystery? Are we to have any gratitude for the positive miracles of life? We thank a man for passing the mustard; is there indeed nothing that we can thank for the man who passes it?

—Excerpt from *Daily News*, June 20, 1903

For the march of scientific progress has brought us only to this: that we have to ask for things that are homely as if they were heroic, and to be won only by heroic virtues. . . . This is the modern achievement: that a human being may yet suffer in order to remain a sane man as a man once suffered to be a saint or martyr. And a man may wage wars to become a peasant as many a man has waged them to become a king.

—Excerpt from *New Witness*, June 14, 1917

Modern men have utterly lost the joy of life. They have to put up with the miserable substitute of the joys of life. And even these they seem less and less able to enjoy. Unless we can make ordinary men interested in ordinary life, we are under the vulgar despotism of those who cannot interest them, but can at least amuse them. Unless we can make daybreak and daily bread and the creative secrets of labor interesting in themselves, there will fall on all our civilization a fatigue, which is the one disease from which civilizations do not recover. So died the great Pagan civilization; of bread and circuses and forgetfulness of the household gods.

—Excerpt from "Seven Days Hard," Broadcast talk, 1934

We may not believe in sacraments, as we may not believe in spirits, but it is quite clear that Christ believed in this sacrament [marriage] in his own way and not in any current or contemporary way. He certainly did not get his argument against divorce from Mosaic law or the Roman law or the habits of the Palestinian people. It would appear to his critics then exactly what it appears to his critics now; an arbitrary and transcendental dogma coming from nowhere save in the sense that it came from him . . . the point here is that it is just as easy to defend that dogma now as it was to defend it then. It is an ideal altogether outside time; difficult at any period; impossible at no period.

—Excerpt from "The Riddles of the Gospel,"
The Everlasting Man

I believe in the brotherhood of men; I also believe in the communion of saints. It so happens that in the street today one of these is called a truism and the other called a dogma. But to me they are both dogmatic and both true.

—Excerpt from *Daily News*, June 3, 1905

꘎

For at present we all tend to one mistake; we tend to make politics too important. We tend to forget how huge a part of a man's life is the same under a Sultan and a Senate, under Nero or Saint Louis.[3] Daybreak is a never-ending glory, getting out of bed is a never-ending nuisance; food and friends will be welcomed; work and strangers must be accepted and endured; birds will go bedwards and children won't, to the end of the last evening. And the worst peril is that in our just modern revolt against intolerable accidents we may have unsettled those things that alone make daily life tolerable. It will be an ironic tragedy if, when we have toiled to find rest, we find we are incurably restless. It will be sad if, when we have worked for our holiday, we find we have unlearnt everything but work.

The typical modern man is the insane millionaire who has drudged to get money, and then finds he cannot enjoy even money. There is danger that the social reformer may silently and occultly develop some of the madness of the millionaire whom he denounces. He may find that he has learnt how to build playgrounds, but forgotten how to play. He may agitate for peace and quiet, but only propagate his own mental agitation. In his long fight to have a half-holiday, he may angrily deny those ancient and natural things—the zest of being, the divinity of man, the sacredness of simple things, the health and humor of the earth—which alone make a half-holiday even half a holiday or a slave even half a man.

—Excerpt from "What Is Right with the World,"
T. P.'s Weekly, Christmas Number, 1910

Mysticism in its noblest sense; mysticism as it existed in Saint John, and Plato, and Paracelsus,[4] and Sir Thomas Browne,[5] is not an exceptionally dark and secret thing, but an exceptionally luminous and open thing. It is in reality too clear for most of us to comprehend, and too obvious for most of us to see. Such an utterance as the utterance that "God is Love" does in reality overwhelm us like an immeasurable landscape on a clear day, like the light of an intolerable summer sun. We may call it a dark saying, but we have an inward knowledge all the time that it is we who are dark.

It is remarkable to notice, even in daily life, how constant is this impression of the essential rationality of mysticism. If we went up to a man in the street who happened to be standing opposite a lamppost and addressed him playfully with the words, "Whence did this strange object spring? How did this lean Cyclops with the eye of fire start out of unbegotten night?" it may generally be inferred, with every possible allowance for the temperament of the individual, that he would not regard our remarks as particularly cogent and practical. And yet our surprise at the lamppost would be entirely rational; his habit of taking lampposts for granted would be merely a superstition.

The power that makes men accept material phenomena of this universe—its cities, civilizations, and solar systems—is merely a vulgar prejudice, like the prejudice which made them accept cockfights or the Inquisition. It is the mystic to whom every star is like a sudden rocket, every flower an earthquake of the dust, who is the clear-minded man. Mysticism, or a sense of the mystery of things, is simply the most gigantic form of common sense. We should not have to complain of any materialism if common sense were only common.

—Excerpt from *Daily News*, August 30, 1901

———— ❦ ————

All true friendliness begins with fire and food and drink and the recognition of rain or frost. . . . Each human soul has in a sense to enact for itself the gigantic humility of the Incarnation. Every man must descend into the flesh to meet mankind.

—Excerpt from "Wisdom and the Weather,"
What's Wrong with the World

⊷

In this world, men frequently try all the odd things before they think of the ordinary thing.

—Excerpt from *New Witness*, December 23, 1921

⊷

Of course, sane people always thought the aim of marriage was the procreation of children to the glory of God.

—Excerpt from "What Is Eugenics?" *Eugenics and Other Evils*

⊷

False science and quack psychology is being used to destroy that natural authority and Christian tradition of the home.

—Excerpt from *New Witness*, August 26, 1921

⊷

The Holy Family is in danger of insult; not even because it is holy, but merely because it is a family.

—Excerpt from *New Witness*, December 10, 1920

———— ❧ ————

It is a good thing for a man to live in a family for the same reason that it is a good thing for a man to be besieged in a city. It is a good thing for a man to live in a family in the same sense that it is a beautiful and delightful thing for a man to be snowed up in a street. They all force him to realize that life is not a thing from outside, but a thing from inside. Above all, they all insist upon the fact that life, if it be a truly stimulating and fascinating life, is a thing which, of its nature, exists in spite of ourselves.

The modern writers who have suggested, in a more or less open manner, that the family is a bad institution, have generally confined themselves to suggesting, with much sharpness, bitterness, or pathos, that perhaps the family is not always very congenial. Of course the family is a good institution because it is uncongenial. It is wholesome precisely because it contains so many divergencies and varieties. It is, as the sentimentalists say, like a little kingdom, and, like most other little kingdoms, is generally in a state of something resembling anarchy. It is exactly because our brother George is not interested in our religious difficulties, but is interested in the Trocadero Restaurant, that the family has some of the bracing qualities of the commonwealth. It is precisely because our uncle Henry does not approve of the theatrical ambitions of our sister Sarah that the family is like humanity. The men and women who, for good reasons and bad, revolt against the family, are, for good reasons and bad, simply revolting against mankind. Aunt Elizabeth is unreasonable, like mankind. Papa is excitable, like mankind. Our youngest brother is mischievous, like mankind. Grandpapa is stupid, like the world; he is old, like the world.

Those who wish, rightly or wrongly, to step out of all this, do definitely wish to step into a narrower world. They are dismayed and terrified by the largeness and variety of the family. Sarah wishes to find a world wholly consisting of private theatricals; George wishes to think the Trocadero a cosmos. I do not say, for a moment, that the flight to this narrower life may not be the right thing for the individual, any more than I say the same thing about flight into a monastery. But I do say that anything is bad and artificial which tends to make these people succumb to the strange delusion that they are stepping into a world which is actually larger and more varied than their own. The best way that a man could test his readiness to encounter the common variety of mankind would be to climb down a chimney into any house at random, and get on as well as possible with the people inside. And that is essentially what each one of us did on the day that he was born.

This is, indeed, the sublime and special romance of the family. It is romantic because it is a toss-up. It is romantic because it is everything that its enemies call it. It is romantic because it is arbitrary. It is romantic because it is there. So long as you have groups of men chosen rationally, you have some special or sectarian atmosphere. It is when you have groups of men chosen irrationally that you have men. The element of adventure begins to exist; for an adventure is, by its nature, a thing that comes to us. It is a thing that chooses us, not a thing that we choose.

Falling in love has been often regarded as the supreme adventure, the supreme romantic accident. In so much as there is in it something outside ourselves, something of a sort of merry fatalism, this is very true. Love does take us and transfigure and torture us. It does break our hearts with an unbearable beauty, like the unbearable beauty of music. But insofar as we have certainly something to do with the matter; insofar as we are in some sense prepared to fall in love and in some sense jump into it; insofar as we do to some extent choose and to some extent even judge—in all this, falling in love is not truly romantic, is not truly adventurous at all. In this degree the supreme adventure is not falling in love. The supreme adventure is being born.

There we do walk suddenly into a splendid and startling trap. There we do see something of which we have not dreamed before. Our father and mother do lie in wait for us and leap out on us, like brigands from a bush. Our uncle is a surprise. Our aunt is, in the beautiful common expression, a bolt from the blue. When we step into the family, by the act of being born, we do step into a world which is incalculable, into a world which has its own strange laws, into a world which could do without us, into a world that we have not made. In other words, when we step into the family we step into a fairy-tale.

—Excerpt from "On Certain Modern Writers
and the Institution of the Family," *Heretics*

Our civilization has decided, and very justly decided, that determining the guilt or innocence of men is a thing too important to be trusted to trained men. It wishes for light upon that awful matter, it asks men who know no more law than I know, but who can feel the things that I felt in the jury box. When it wants a library catalogued, or the solar system discovered, or any trifle of that kind, it uses up its specialists. But when it wishes anything done which is really serious, it collects twelve of the ordinary men standing round. The same thing was done, if I remember right, by the Founder of Christianity.

—Excerpt from "The Twelve Men," *Tremendous Trifles*

He who has gone back to the beginning, and seen everything as quaint and new, will always see things in their right order, the one depending on the other in degree of purpose and importance: the poker for the fire and the fire for the man and the man for the glory of God.

—Excerpt from "The Man Who Thinks Backwards,"
A Miscellany of Men

Men need a religion primarily to prevent them from worshiping idols.

—Excerpt from *Illustrated London News*, June 20, 1914

People sometimes wonder how men come to fight about their opinions; to fight until blood runs down the gutters. The explanation is really quite simple; it is that any dispute between any two disputants becomes ultimately a dispute about common sense. And they always discover that common sense is the one thing that they have not got in common. The great misfortune of common sense is that it is altogether a spiritual thing. Nay, common sense is even a celestial thing; common sense is not of this world. One can tell the divine origin of common sense by this simple test; that it is always crucified.

—Excerpt from *Daily News,* March 16, 1907

Through ages in which the most arrogant and elaborate ideals of power and civilization held otherwise undisputed sway, the ideal of the perfect and healthy peasant did undoubtedly represent in some shape or form the conception that there was a dignity in simplicity and a dignity in labor. It was good for the ancient aristocrat, even if he could not attain to innocence and the wisdom of the earth, to believe that these things were the secrets of the priesthood of the poor. It was good for him to believe that even if heaven was not above him, heaven was below him. It was well that he should have, amid all his flamboyant triumphs, the never-extinguished sentiment that there was something better than his triumphs, the conception that "there remaineth a rest."

The conception of the Ideal Shepherd seems absurd to our modern ideas. But, after all, it was perhaps the only trade of the democracy which was equalized with the trades of the aristocracy even by the aristocracy itself. The shepherd of pastoral poetry was, without doubt, very different from the shepherd of actual fact. Where one innocently piped to his lambs, the other innocently swore at them; and their divergence in intellect and personal cleanliness was immense. But the difference between the ideal shepherd who danced with Amaryllis[6] and the real shepherd who thrashed her is not a scrap greater than the difference between the ideal soldier who dies to capture the colors and the real soldier who lives to clean his accoutrements, between the ideal priest who is everlastingly by someone's bed and the real priest who is as glad as anyone else to get to his own. There are ideal conceptions and real men in every calling; yet there are few who object to the ideal conceptions, and not many, after all, who object to the real men.

The fact, then, is this: so far from resenting the existence in art and literature of an ideal shepherd, I genuinely regret that the shepherd is the only democratic calling that has ever been raised to the level of the heroic callings conceived by an aristocratic age. So far from objecting to the Ideal Shepherd, I wish there were an Ideal Postman, an Ideal Grocer, and an Ideal Plumber. It is undoubtedly true that we should laugh at the idea of an Ideal Postman; it is true, and it proves that we are not genuine democrats.

Undoubtedly the modern grocer, if called upon to act in an Arcadian manner, if desired to oblige with a symbolic dance expressive of the delights of grocery, or to perform on some simple instrument while his assistants skipped around him, would be embarrassed, and perhaps even reluctant. But it may be questioned whether this temporary reluctance of the grocer is a good thing, or evidence of a good condition of poetic feeling in the grocery business as a whole. There certainly should be an ideal image of health and happiness in any trade, and its remoteness from the reality is not the only important question. No one supposes that the mass of traditional conceptions of duty and glory are always operative, for example, in the mind of a soldier or a doctor; that the Battle of Waterloo actually makes a private enjoy pipeclaying his trousers,[7] or that the "health of humanity" softens the momentary phraseology of a physician called out of bed at two o'clock in the morning. But although no ideal obliterates the ugly drudgery and detail of any calling, that ideal does, in the case of the soldier or the doctor, exist definitely in the background and makes that drudgery worthwhile as a whole. It is a serious calamity that no such ideal exists in the case of the vast number of honorable trades and crafts on which the existence of a modern city depends. It is a pity that current thought and sentiment offer nothing corresponding to the old conception of patron saints. If they did, there would be a Patron Saint of Plumbers, and this would alone be a revolution, for it would force the individual craftsman to believe that there was once a perfect being who did actually plumb.

When all is said and done, then, we think it much open to question whether the world has not lost something in the complete disappearance of the ideal of the happy peasant. It is foolish enough to suppose that the rustic went about all over ribbons, but it is better than knowing that he goes about all over rags and being indifferent to the fact. The modern realistic study of the poor does in reality lead the student further astray than the old idyllic notion. For we cannot get the chiaroscuro[8] of humble life so long as its virtues seem to us as gross as its vices, and its joys as sullen as its sorrows. Probably at the very moment that we can see nothing but a dull-faced man smoking and drinking heavily with his friend in a pothouse,[9] the man himself is on his soul's holiday, crowned with the flowers of a passionate idleness, and far more like the Happy Peasant than the world will ever know.

—Excerpt from "A Defence of China Shepherdesses,"
The Defendant

If no one should be left in the world except a million open malefactors and one hypocrite, that hypocrite will still remind them of holiness.

—Excerpt from *Daily News,* November 10, 1906

A man will not roll in the snow for a stream of tendency by which all things fulfill the law of their being. He will not go without food in the name of something, not ourselves, that makes for righteousness. He will do things like this, or pretty nearly like this, under quite a different impulse. He will do these things when he is in love.

The first fact to realize about Saint Francis is . . . he was a lover. He was a lover of God and he was really and truly a lover of men; possibly a much rarer mystical vocation. A lover of men is very nearly the opposite of a philanthropist; indeed the pedantry of the Greek word carries something like a satire on itself. A philanthropist may be said to love anthropoids. But as Saint Francis did not love humanity but men, so he did not love Christianity but Christ. Say, if you think so, that he was a lunatic loving an imaginary person; but an imaginary person, not an imaginary idea. And for the modern reader the clue to the asceticism and all the rest can best be found in the stories of lovers when they seemed to be rather like lunatics. Tell it as the tale of one of the

Troubadours,[10] and the wild things he would do for his lady, and the whole of the modern puzzle disappears. In such a romance there would be no contradiction between the poet gathering flowers in the sun and enduring a freezing vigil in the snow, between his praising all earthly and bodily beauty and then refusing to eat, between his glorifying gold and purple and perversely going in rags, between his showing pathetically a hunger for a happy life and a thirst for a heroic death. All these riddles would easily be resolved in the simplicity of any noble love; only this was so noble a love that nine men out of ten have hardly even heard of it. We shall see later that this parallel of the earthly lover has a very practical relation to the problems of his life, as to his relations with his father and with his friends and their families. The modern reader will almost always find that if he could only feel this kind of love as a reality, he could feel this kind of extravagance as a romance. But I only note . . . that to this great mystic his religion was not a thing like a theory, but a thing like a love affair.

—Excerpt from "The Problem of Saint Francis,"
Saint Francis of Assisi

It may seem a paradox to say that a man may be transported with joy to discover that he is in debt. But this is only because in commercial cases the creditor does not generally share the transports of joy; especially when the debt is by hypothesis infinite and therefore unrecoverable. But, here again, the parallel of a natural love story of the nobler sort disposes of the difficulty in a flash. There the infinite creditor does share the joy of the infinite debtor, for indeed they are both debtors and both creditors. In other words, debt and dependence do become pleasures in the presence of unspoiled love; the word is used too loosely and luxuriously in popular simplifications like the present, but here the word is really the key. It is the key to all the problems of Franciscan morality which puzzle the merely modern mind; but above all it is the key to asceticism. It is the highest and holiest of the paradoxes that the man who really knows he cannot pay his debt will be forever paying it. He will be forever giving back what he cannot give back, and cannot be expected to give back. He will be always throwing things away into a bottomless pit of unfathomable thanks. Men who think they are too modern to understand this are in fact too mean to understand it; we are most of us too mean to practice it. We are not generous enough to be ascetics; one might almost say not genial enough to be ascetics. A man must have magnanimity of surrender, of which he commonly only catches a glimpse in first love, like a glimpse of our lost Eden. But whether he sees it or not, the truth is in that riddle, that the whole world has, or is, only one good thing; and it is a bad debt.

If ever that rarer sort of romantic love, which was the truth that sustained the Troubadours, falls out of fashion and is treated as fiction, we may see some such misunderstanding as that of the modern world about asceticism. For it seems conceivable that some barbarians might try to destroy chivalry in love, as the barbarians ruling in Berlin destroyed chivalry in war. If that were ever so, we should have the same sort of unintelligent sneers and unimaginative questions. Men will ask what selfish sort of woman it must have been who ruthlessly exacted tribute in the form of flowers, or what an avaricious creature she could have been to demand solid gold in the form of a ring, just as they ask what cruel kind of God can have demanded sacrifice and self-denial. They will have lost the clue to all that lovers have meant by love and will not understand that it was because the thing was not demanded that it was done.

—Excerpt from "Le Jongleur de Dieu,"
Saint Francis of Assisi

꘎

The hagiological[11] way is the logical way, though its embodiments may seem extreme and startling, as logical things often do.

—Excerpt from *New Witness*, May 17, 1918

VIII

Joy: the Gigantic Secret of the Christian

I feel an almost savage envy on hearing that London has been flooded in my absence . . . Battersea[1] must be a vision of Venice. . . .

Some consider such romantic views of flood or fire slightly lacking in reality. But really this romantic view of such inconveniences is quite as practical as the other. The true optimist who sees in such things an opportunity for enjoyment is quite as logical and much more sensible than the ordinary "Indignant Ratepayer" who sees in them an opportunity for grumbling. Real pain, as in the case of being burnt at Smithfield[2] or having a toothache, is a positive thing; it can be supported, but scarcely enjoyed. But, after all, our toothaches are the exception, and as for being burnt at Smithfield, it only happens to us at the very longest intervals. And most of the inconveniences that make men swear or women cry are really sentimental or imaginative inconveniences—things altogether of the mind.

For instance, we often hear grown-up people complaining of having to hang about a railway station and wait for a train. Did you ever hear a small boy complain of having to hang about a railway station and wait for a train? No, for to him to be inside a railway station is to be inside a cavern of wonder and a palace of poetical pleasures. Because to him the red light and the green light on the signal are like a new sun and a new moon. Because to him when the wooden arm of the signal falls down suddenly, it is as if a great king had thrown down his staff as a signal and started a shrieking tournament of trains. I myself am of little boys' habit in this matter. They also serve who only stand and wait for the two fifteen. Their meditations may be full of rich and fruitful things. Many of the most purple hours of my life[3] have been passed at Clapham Junction, which is now, I suppose, under water. I have been there in many moods so fixed and mystical that the water might well have come up to my waist before I noticed it particularly. But in the case of all such annoyances, as I have said, everything depends upon the emotional point of view. You can safely apply the test to almost every one of the things that are currently talked of as the typical nuisance of daily life.

For instance, there is a current impression that it is unpleasant to have to run after one's hat. Why should it be unpleasant to the well-ordered and pious mind? Not merely because it is running, and running exhausts one. The same people run much faster in games and sports. The same people run much more eagerly after an uninteresting little leather ball than they will after a nice silk hat. There is an idea that it is humiliating to run after one's hat; and when people say it is humiliating they mean that it is comic. It certainly is comic; but man is a very comic creature, and most of the things he does are comic—eating, for instance. And the most comic things of all are exactly the things that are most worth doing—such as making love. . . .

Now a man could, if he felt rightly in the matter, run after his hat with the manliest ardor and the most sacred joy. He might regard himself as a jolly huntsman pursuing a wild animal, for certainly no animal could be wilder. In fact, I am inclined to believe that hat hunting on windy days will be the sport of the upper classes in the future. There will be a meet of ladies and gentlemen on some high ground on a gusty morning. They will be told that the professional attendants have started a hat in such-and-such a thicket, or whatever be the technical term. Notice that this employment will in the fullest degree combine sport with humanitarianism. The hunters would feel that they were not inflicting pain. Nay, they would feel that they were inflicting pleasure—rich, almost riotous pleasure—upon the people who were looking on. When last I saw an old gentleman running after his hat in Hyde Park, I told him that a heart so benevolent as his ought to be filled with peace and thanks at the thought of how much unaffected pleasure his every gesture and bodily attitude were at that moment giving to the crowd.

The same principle can be applied to every other typical domestic worry. A gentleman trying to get a fly out of the milk or a piece of cork out of his glass of wine often imagines himself to be irritated. Let him think for a moment of the patience of anglers sitting by dark pools, and let his soul be immediately irradiated with gratification and repose. Again, I have known some people of very modern views driven by their distress to the use of theological terms to which they attached no doctrinal significance, merely because a drawer was jammed tight and they could not pull it out. A friend of mine was particularly afflicted in this way. Every day his drawer was jammed, and every day in consequence it was something else that rhymes with it [jam]. But I pointed out to him that this sense of wrong was really subjective and relative; it rested entirely upon the assumption that the drawer could, should, and would come out easily. "But if," I said, "you picture to yourself that you are pulling against some powerful and oppressive enemy, the struggle will become merely exciting and not exasperating. Imagine that you are tugging up a lifeboat out of the sea. Imagine that you are roping up a fellow creature out of an alpine crevasse. Imagine even that you are a boy again and engaged in a tug-of-war between French and English." Shortly after saying this I left him; but I have no doubt at all that my words bore the best possible fruit. I have no doubt that every day of his life he hangs on to the handle of that drawer with a flushed face and eyes bright with battle, uttering encouraging shouts to himself, and seeming to hear all round him the roar of an applauding ring.

So I do not think that it is altogether fanciful or incredible to suppose that even the floods in London may be accepted and enjoyed poetically. Nothing beyond inconvenience seems really to have been caused by them; and inconvenience, as I have said, is only one aspect, and that the most unimaginative and accidental aspect of a really romantic situation. An adventure is only an inconvenience rightly considered. An inconvenience is only an adventure wrongly considered.

—Excerpt from "On Running After One's Hat,"
All Things Considered

We are to regard existence as a raid or great adventure; it is to be judged, therefore, not by what calamities it encounters, but by what flag it follows and what high town it assaults. The most dangerous thing in the world is to be alive; one is always in danger of one's life. But anyone who shrinks from this is a traitor to the great scheme and experiment of being.

—Excerpt from "What Is Right with the World,"
T. P.'s Weekly, Christmas Number, 1910

If there are ghastly things to be faced the only thing we can do is make it glorious to face them.

—Excerpt from *New Witness*, May 17, 1918

Life is serious all the time; but living cannot be serious all the time. . . . In anything that does cover the whole of your life—in your philosophy and your religion—you must have mirth. If you do not have mirth you will certainly have madness.

—Excerpt from *Daily News,* September 1, 1906

If the whole world was suddenly stricken with a sense of humor it would find itself mechanically fulfilling the Sermon on the Mount.

—Excerpt from "Tolstoy and the Cult of Simplicity,"
Varied Types

Humor is meant, in a literal sense, to make game of man; that is, to dethrone him from his official dignity and hunt him like game. It is meant to remind us human beings that we have things about us as ungainly and ludicrous as the nose of the elephant or the neck of the giraffe. If laughter does not touch a sort of fundamental folly, it does not do its duty in bringing us back to an enormous and original simplicity. Nothing has been worse than the modern notion that a clever man can make a joke without taking part in it; without sharing in the general absurdity that such a situation creates. It is unpardonable conceit not to laugh at your own jokes. Joking is undignified; that is why it is so good for one's soul.

—Excerpt from "The Flat Freak," *Alarms and Discursions*

Laughter has something in it in common with the ancient winds of faith and inspiration; it unfreezes pride and unwinds secrecy; it makes men forget themselves in the presence of something greater than themselves; something (as the common phrase goes about a joke) that they cannot resist.

—Excerpt from "Laughter," *The Common Man*

———— ❧ ————

Whatever is cosmic is comic.

—Excerpt from "Spiritualism,"*All Things Considered*

———— ❧ ————

The secret of life lies in laughter and humility.

—Excerpt from "The Moods of Mr. George Moore," *Heretics*

———— ❧ ————

It is the test of a good religion whether you can joke about it.

—Excerpt from "Spiritualism," *All Things Considered*

———— ❧ ————

A man must have some real joy in him before he can become a martyr.

—Excerpt from *Daily News,* June 7, 1901

The soul might be rapt out of the body in an agony of sorrow, or a trance of ecstasy, but it might also be rapt out of the body in a paroxysm of laughter.

—Excerpt from "A Midsummer Night's Dream,"
Chesterton on Shakespeare

The element of fear is one of the eternal ingredients of joy. The faculty of being shy is the first and the most delicate of the powers of enjoyment. The fear of the Lord is the beginning of pleasure.

—Excerpt from *Daily News*, December 5, 1901

The grand old defiers of God were not afraid of an eternity of torment. We have come to be afraid of an eternity of joy.

—Excerpt from "The Pickwick Papers," *Charles Dickens*

The one most exalted and enthusiastic mood, merely considered as a mood, is that of the man who can affirm and witness to a truth above all his moods. To enjoy this, a man must have a philosophy. But the narrow philosophy is that which only allows of one mood, such as rebellion, or disdain, or even despair. The large philosophy is that which allows of many moods; such as charity, or zeal, or patience. And it is so with what I count the largest of philosophies; which can be in revolt against the Prince of the World while it is loyal to the creator of the World; which can love the world like Saint Francis, or renounce the world like Saint Jerome. The point is that the Christian not only has mirth and indignation and compassion and comradeship and individual isolation; but he has them consistently; and each of them has a clear place in his theory of things.

—Excerpt from *New Witness*, October 15, 1920

Melancholy is a frivolous thing compared with the seriousness of joy. Melancholy is negative; it has to do with trivialities like death. Joy is positive and has to answer for the renewal and perpetuation of being. Melancholy is irresponsible; it could watch the universe fall to pieces. Joy is responsible and upholds the universe in the void of space.

—Excerpt from *Daily News,* June 11, 1901

It might reasonably be maintained that the true object of all human life is play. Earth is a task garden; heaven is a playground. To be at last in such secure innocence that one can juggle with the universe and the stars, to be so good that one can treat everything as a joke—that may be, perhaps, the real end and final holiday of human souls. When we are really holy we may regard the Universe as a lark.

—Excerpt from "Oxford from Without,"
All Things Considered

The whole difference between philosophy and religion is expressed in this: it is the difference between the very small section of people who can understand things and the very large number who can enjoy them.

—Excerpt from *Daily News,* May 30, 1903

Great joy has in it the sense of immortality; the triumphant moments of our life may have been only moments, but they were moments of eternity.

—Excerpt from *Daily News,* March 7, 1901

It is said that Paganism is a religion of joy and Christianity of sorrow; it would be just as easy to prove that Paganism is pure sorrow and Christianity pure joy. Such conflicts mean nothing and lead nowhere. Everything human must have in it both joy and sorrow; the only matter of interest is the manner in which the two things are balanced or divided. And the really interesting thing is this—that the pagan was (in the main) happier and happier as he approached the earth, but sadder and sadder as he approached the heavens. The gaiety of the best Paganism, as in the playfulness of Catullus or Theocritus,[4] is, indeed, an eternal gaiety never to be forgotten by a grateful humanity. But it is all a gaiety about the facts of life, not about its origin. To the pagan the small things are as sweet as the small brooks breaking out of the mountain; but the broad things are as bitter as the sea. When the pagan looks at the very core of the cosmos he is struck cold. Behind the gods, who are merely despotic, sit the fates, who are deadly. Nay, the fates are worse than deadly; they are dead.

And when rationalists say that the ancient world was more enlightened than the Christian, from their point of view they are right. For when they say "enlightened" they mean darkened with incurable despair. It is profoundly true that the ancient world was more modern than the Christian. The common bond is in the fact that ancients and moderns have both been miserable about existence, about everything, while mediaevals were happy about that at least. I freely grant that the pagans, like the moderns, were only miserable about everything—they were quite jolly about everything else. I concede that the Christians of the Middle Ages were only at peace about everything—they were at war about everything else. But if the question turns on the primary pivot of the cosmos, then there was more cosmic contentment in the narrow and bloody streets of Florence than in the theater of Athens or the open garden of Epicurus. Giotto lived in a gloomier town than Euripides,[5] but he lived in a gayer universe.

The mass of men have been forced to be gay about the little things, but sad about the big ones. Nevertheless (I offer my last dogma defiantly) it is not native to man to be so. Man is more himself, man is more manlike, when joy is the fundamental thing in him, and grief the superficial. Melancholy should be an innocent interlude, a tender and fugitive frame of mind; praise should be the permanent pulsation of the soul. Pessimism is at best an emotional half-holiday; joy is the uproarious labor by which all things live.

Yet, according to the apparent estate of man as seen by the pagan or the agnostic, this primary need of human nature can never be fulfilled. Joy ought to be expansive; but for the agnostic it must be contracted, it must cling to one corner of the world. Grief ought to be a concentration; but for the agnostic its desolation is spread through an unthinkable eternity. This is what I call being born upside down. The skeptic may truly be said to be topsy-turvy; for his feet are dancing upwards in idle ecstasies, while his brain is in the abyss. To the modern man the heavens are actually below the earth. The explanation is simple: he is standing on his head, which is a very weak pedestal to stand on. But when he has found his feet again he knows it. Christianity satisfies suddenly and perfectly man's ancestral instinct for being the right way up; satisfies it supremely in this: that, by its creed, joy becomes something gigantic and sadness something special and small. The vault above us is not deaf because the universe is an idiot; the silence is not the heartless silence of an endless and aimless world. Rather the silence around us is a small and pitiful stillness like the prompt stillness in a sick room. We are perhaps permitted tragedy as a sort of merciful comedy: because the frantic energy of divine things would knock us down like a drunken farce. We can take our own tears more lightly than we could take the tremendous levities of the angels. So we sit perhaps in a starry chamber of silence, while the laughter of the heavens is too loud for us to hear.

Joy, which was the small publicity of the pagan, is the gigantic secret of the Christian. And as I close this chaotic volume I open again the strange small book from which all Christianity came; and I am again haunted by a kind of confirmation. The tremendous figure which fills the Gospels towers in this respect, as in every other, above all the thinkers who ever thought themselves tall. His pathos was natural, almost casual. The Stoics, ancient and modern, were proud of concealing their tears. He never concealed his tears; He showed them plainly on his open face at any daily sight, such as the far sight of his native city. Yet he concealed something. Solemn supermen and imperial diplomatists are proud of restraining their anger. He never restrained his anger. He flung furniture down the front steps of the Temple, and asked men how they expected to escape the damnation of hell. Yet he restrained something. I say it with reverence; there was in that shattering personality a thread that must be called shyness. There was something that he hid from all men when he went up a mountain to pray. There was something that he covered constantly by abrupt silence or impetuous isolation. There was some one thing that was too great for God to show us when he walked upon our earth; and I have sometimes fancied that it was his mirth.

—Excerpt from "Authority and the Adventurer," *Orthodoxy*

Editor's Notes

Chapter I

1. "But if God so clothes the grass of the field, which is alive today and tomorrow is thrown into the oven, will he not much more clothe you—you of little faith?" (Matthew 6:30).

2. Chesterton is referring to "A Squire's Tale" in Geoffrey Chaucer's *Canterbury Tales*.

Chapter II

1. The ancient Greek philosophy of Stoicism held that the wise man or sage acted only according to reason, stamping out all passions so as to endure any discomfort.

2. Julian the Apostate (d. 363) was a Roman emperor who rejected Christianity and tried to restore paganism as the state religion. Julian attempted to reverse his baptism by bathing in a bull's blood.

Chapter IV

1. Cheapside is a street in a famous shopping district of London.

2. Athene, Greek goddess of reason; Artemis, Greek goddess of chastity, virginity, the hunt; Vesta, Roman goddess of the home and fire.

3. The Manichees followed a dualistic religion that saw matter as evil.

4. Arthur Schopenhauer (1788–1860) was a German atheistic philosopher.

5. Chesterton is speaking of his own cultural customs; in some East Asian cultures white is traditionally worn at funerals. They have only recently been influenced by Western culture in the wearing of black to funerals.

Chapter V

1. Probably refers to the third-century Christian writer Tertullian, since the Latin phrase is derived from his work *De Carne Christi,* though it is not an exact quote.

2. The *Catechism of Christian Doctrine,* a popular catechism in Britain for many years. It originally sold for a penny.

3. The saturnalia was an ancient Roman festival held in December in honor of the deity Saturn.

Chapter VII

1. A Tory was a member of the British political party that opposed the exclusion of James, Duke of York, from royal succession (1679–80). Tory remained the name for major conservative interests until they gave birth to the Conservative Party in the 1830s.

2. Giotto di Bondone (c. 1266–1337), known as Giotto, was an Italian painter and architect from Florence. He is generally considered the first in a line of great artists who contributed to the Renaissance. Blessed Fra Angelico (or Guido di Pietro, c. 1385–1455) was an Italian Dominican friar and early Renaissance painter.

3. Louis IX (1214–1270) was a Capetian King of France who reigned from 1226 until his death.

4. Paracelsus was Philip von Hohenheim (1493–1541), a Swiss physician and astrologer who became a folk legend in Europe.

5. Sir Thomas Browne (1605–1682) was an English physician who also wrote religious works.

6. Amaryllis was a spirit of spring often depicted as dancing over flowers and grass with a wreath of flowers in her hair.

7. Pipe clay is a fine, white clay that soldiers would put on their breeches to keep them clean. When it dried the clay would form clouds of dust.

8. Chiaroscuro is the effect of contrasted light and shadow created by light falling unevenly or from a particular direction.

9. A pothouse is another name for a small tavern.

10. Troubadours were French medieval lyric poets in the eleventh to thirteenth centuries, who performed songs on the theme of courtly love.

11. Hagiological—relating to the saints or their writings.

Chapter VIII

1. Battersea is located in an area of south London that is prone to flooding.

2. Smithfield is an area in London where people were executed, especially in medieval times.

3. Colors were very symbolic for Chesterton. Perhaps by "purple hour" he was thinking of what he said of that color in *What's Wrong with the World:* "Purple, at once rich and somber, does suggest a triumph temporarily eclipsed by a tragedy."

4. Gaius Valerius Catullus (c. 84–54 BC) was a Latin poet of the late Roman Republic who wrote vividly about human emotions. Theocritus (c. 300–c. 260) was a Greek poet who originated the genre of pastoral poetry with his bucolic idylls.

5. Euripides (c. 480–406 BC) was a famous playwright of Greek tragedies.

Bibliography

BOOKS

Ahlquist, Dale, editor. *The Soul of Wit: G. K. Chesterton on William Shakespeare*. Mineola, NY: Dover, 2012.

Chesterton, G. K. *Alarms and Discursions*. London: Methuen, 1910.

———. *All Things Considered*. London: Methuen, 1908.

———. *The Apostle and the Wild Ducks*. London: Paul Elek, 1975.

———. *As I Was Saying*. London: Methuen, 1936.

———. *Autobiography*. London: Hutchinson. 1936.

———. *The Ball and the Cross*. New York: John Lane, 1909.

———. *William Blake*. London: Duckworth, 1910.

———. *Charles Dickens*. London: Methuen, 1906.

———. *Chaucer*. London: Faber and Faber, 1932.

———. *The Coloured Lands*. London: Sheed and Ward, 1938.

———. *Come to Think of It*. London: Methuen, 1930.

———. *The Common Man*. London: Sheed and Ward, 1950.

———. *The Crimes of England*. London: Cecil Palmer, 1915.

———. *The Defendant*. London: R. Brimley Johnson, 1902.

———. *Eugenics and Other Evils*. London: Cassell, 1922.

———. *The Everlasting Man*. London: Hodder and Stoughton, 1925.

———. *G. F. Watts*. London: Duckworth, 1904.

———. *George Bernard Shaw*. London: John Lane, 1909.

———. *Heretics*. London: John Lane, 1905.

———. *Irish Impressions*. London: W. Collins Sons, 1919.

———. *The Man Who Knew Too Much*. London: Cassell, 1922.

———. *A Miscellany of Men*. London: Methuen, 1912.

———. *The Napoleon of Notting Hill*. London: John Lane, 1904.

———. *The New Jerusalem*. London: Hodder and Stoughton, 1920.

———. *Orthodoxy*. London: John Lane, 1908.

———. *The Resurrection of Rome*. London: Hodder and Stoughton, 1930.

———. *Robert Louis Stevenson*. London: Hodder and Stoughton, 1927.

———. *A Short History of England*. London: Chatto and Windus. 1917.

———. *Sidelights on New London and Newer York*. London: Sheed and Ward, 1932.

———. *The Spice of Life*. Beaconsfield: Darwen Finlayson, 1964.

———. *Saint Francis of Assisi*. London: Hodder and Stoughton, 1923.

———. *Saint Thomas Aquinas*. London: Hodder and Stoughton, 1933.

———. *The Thing*. London: Sheed and Ward, 1929.

———. *Tremendous Trifles. London*: Methuen. 1909.

———. *What's Wrong with the World*. London: Cassell, 1910.

———. *Where All Roads Lead*. London: Catholic Truth Society, 1961.

———. *Varied Types*. New York: Dodd, Mead, 1903.

PERIODICALS

America

The Bibliophile

The Bookman

The Clarion

Columbia

Daily News

Dublin Review

The Listener

Hearst's Magazine

Illustrated London News

Our Sunday Visitor

New Witness

New York American

The Speaker

T. P.'s Weekly

The Tribune

OTHER

Chesterton, G. K. *Divorce versus Democracy*. London: Society of SS. Peter and Paul, 1916.

The Book of Job. Introduction to by G. K. Chesterton. New York: Dodge, 1909.

Dickens, Charles. *Dombey and Son*. Introduction by G. K. Chesterton. New York: J. M. Dent, 1907.

Dickens, Charles. *Pickwick Papers*. Introduction by G. K. Chesterton. New York: J. M. Dent, 1907.

Thackeray. Introduction by G. K. Chesterton, editor. London: George Bell and Sons, 1909.

Ward, Maise. *Gilbert Keith Chesterton.* Quoting "Letter to Frances." London: Sheed and Ward, 1943.

"The Fanatic." Reprinted in *The Collected Works of G. K. Chesterton*, Volume X, Part I. San Francisco: Ignatius Press. 1994.

BOOKS & MEDIA

A mission of the Daughters of St. Paul

As apostles of Jesus Christ, evangelizing today's world:

We are CALLED to holiness
by God's living Word and Eucharist.

We COMMUNICATE the Gospel message
through our lives and through all
available forms of media.

We SERVE the Church
by responding to the hopes and needs
of all people with the Word of God,
in the spirit of St. Paul.

For more information visit www.pauline.org.

BOOKS & MEDIA

The Daughters of St. Paul operate book and media centers at the following addresses. Visit, call, or write the one nearest you today, or find us at www.pauline.org.

CALIFORNIA

3908 Sepulveda Blvd, Culver City, CA 90230   310-397-8676

935 Brewster Avenue, Redwood City, CA 94063   650-369-4230

FLORIDA

145 S.W. 107th Avenue, Miami, FL 33174   305-559-6715

HAWAII

1143 Bishop Street, Honolulu, HI 96813   808-521-2731

ILLINOIS

172 North Michigan Avenue, Chicago, IL 60601   312-346-4228

LOUISIANA

4403 Veterans Memorial Blvd, Metairie, LA 70006   504-887-7631

MASSACHUSETTS

885 Providence Hwy, Dedham, MA 02026   781-326-5385

MISSOURI

9804 Watson Road, St. Louis, MO 63126   314-965-3512

NEW YORK

64 W. 38th Street, New York, NY 10018   212-754-1110

SOUTH CAROLINA

243 King Street, Charleston, SC 29401   843-577-0175

TEXAS

Currently no book center; for parish exhibits or outreach evangelization, contact: 210-569-0500, or SanAntonio@paulinemedia.com, or P.O. Box 761416, San Antonio, TX 78245

VIRGINIA

1025 King Street, Alexandria, VA 22314   703-549-3806

CANADA

3022 Dufferin Street, Toronto, ON M6B 3T5   416-781-9131

¡También somos su fuente para libros,
videos y música en español!